D1049888

# The Resurgent Neighborhood

# THE
# RESURGENT
# NEIGHBORHOOD

## James V. Cunningham

SACRED HEART MONASTERY
LEO BERON
LIBRARY
301.364
HALBIG MALAY MR.

C 917

FIDES PUBLISHERS, INC. • 1965

Notre Dame, Indiana

Copyright © 1965, Fides Publishers, Inc.

Notre Dame, Indiana

Library of Congress Catalog Card Number: 65-16198

*Manufactured in the United States*

# Preface

This book seeks to record experience, conviction, and speculation about the modern urban place. It seeks particularly to show the importance of the neighborhood in today's urban life.

It is based on fifteen years of work with citizens, mostly in the neighborhoods of Chicago and Pittsburgh. Out of this experience has come the conviction that the local neighborhood community, renewed and developed in some new form now about to emerge, has a substantial contribution to make in the lives of urban people. This conviction applies with equal force to inner-city neighborhoods affected by delinquency, poverty, and race tension, and to suburban neighborhoods burdened with monotonous housing and the tensions of status-seeking.

America is shifting from a nation of town and city dwellers to a nation of metropolis dwellers. This environment is at once richer, more complex, and more bewildering than anything we have faced before. Within this complicated new society many forms and levels of community are important for man. The family, the municipality, the metropolis itself, are of great importance. A man's relatives often form a community crucial to his life, as do friends and job colleagues. These do not seem sufficient, however, to relate urban man to the large institutions and power forces of the metropolis, and to give him the support he needs in his day-to-day life.

In addition to being a living area and service district, the neighborhood, reorganized and adapted for contemporary life, holds great potential as a link between man and the metropolis. It has been proving itself the natural

5

unit in which citizens' organizations and government planners can take hold of many urban problems. The urban neighborhood is developing as the most advantageous battleground for winning the war on poverty. It may well be one of the most important communities for modern man.

There are four parts to this book. The first chapter looks at the coming into being of an urban society in which men more and more live in the dwarfing metropolis. Examining the metropolis, and particularly its heart, the central-city core, the Introduction seeks to identify the sources of metropolitan strength and vitality. It looks at the organized movement under way to develop, renew, and improve the metropolis as a prosperous, well-functioning, livable place.

Chapters two and three look at the urban neighborhood, probing its nature, seeing its role in supporting man, looking at its different types, and examining the elements needed to make a strong neighborhood community.

The next six chapters are case studies about specific neighborhoods. These chapters tell the story of people who in recent years have struggled to realize opportunities and overcome obstacles in making their neighborhoods strong local communities. New approaches to neighborhood renewal and development are examined in these chapters. The last four chapters deal critically with emerging new ideas, new resources, and new and competing approaches for developing the urban neighborhood to its full potential, with the final chapter containing a summation and look into the future.

These chapters are intended primarily for the housewife, clergyman, teacher, salesman, architect, factory worker, postal clerk—for people who live in neighborhoods and take the time to read books. Written much more for this wider audience than for urban development professionals, this book aims to provide information and ideas for neighborhood people. The author believes that voluntary participation and creative citizen leadership, joined with competent official action, is the basic key to developing strong urban neighborhoods. The good will and leadership potential of neighborhood people is one of our most important urban assets.

This book seeks to evoke citizen response and comment and to increase citizen attention to the challenge of neighborhood vitalization. It hopes to stimulate more thinking about the purpose of the neighborhood and its relevance to contemporary life.

A number of persons have been of considerable aid in the preparation of this book. Some of those to whom the author is most indebted are: Ozzie Badal, Margaret M. Cunningham, Leon and Marion Despres, B. Burtt Evans, Leslie Gallagher, James Hibbin, Irving Horwitz, Bernard E. Loshbough, Edward Marciniak, B. Warner Shippee, Kiernan F. Stenson and Robert B. Williams.

The author is grateful also to Fides editors Eugene Geissler and John McCudden, and to typist Donalee Voelker. And most of all he acknowledges the patience of his wife, Rita, who endured two years of Saturday-night writing sessions.

Others who have contributed are named in the text itself.

# Contents

# Chapter 1

## THE URBAN RUSH

Worldwide, we have entered the age of urban man. Rural people, made jobless by mechanized, scientific agriculture, weary of hardship and lured by the material and cultural wealth of cities, are pouring into urban places where they are suffering, struggling, and facing unprecedented opportunities for human development.

In the urban places they enter there are already vast swarms of people becoming ever more numerous from high birth rates and the success of modern medicine in conquering disease. Only 150 years ago every nation on the planet was overwhelmingly rural. Today, one-third of the world's three billion people are urban dwellers. There are forty nations with more than half their population living in urban places. By the end of the century, according to the Urban Land Institute, there will be more people living in towns and cities than now live in the entire world: three and a half billion out of six billion.

This is profound and revolutionary change. The focus of man's life is shifting from growing to making, from earth-nature to man-nature, from living with the familiar few to dwelling among the strange many. People and institutions, rather than land and climate, are coming to dominate. Social organization is becoming more complex, politics more harsh and volatile. More is demanded of man, and more is offered him.

In the United States there is a double urban rush: the movement of rural people into the old central cities, and the even greater movement of central-city people outward to the new suburbs around the cities. This double rush reflects the hope and seeking of all men for an improved lot; it reflects the upward thrust for social status in the urban place; and it begets, as we shall see, division and conflict, along with advancement. It tends to leave behind, separated and forgotten, the poor, the Negro, the aged.

An urban place is generally defined as one with a population of two thousand or more. But the typical place to which men are being drawn is the metropolis, a great sprawling urban mass. "Metropolis" is an old Greek word meaning "mother city." In ancient times the term was applied to those few supercities which grew up around a temple, market place, and seat of government. In our day it is increasingly applied to the modern supercity composed of towns and suburbs, commercial and industrial subcenters and old-city neighborhoods clustered around a central core—a Loop, a Golden Triangle, a Manhattan.

This mass of human beings, activity, and property is held together by buying, selling, and jobs; highways, streets, and telephones; banks and department stores; daily newspapers, radio and TV stations; public transit; and a host of common opportunities and problems.

The vast majority of today's urban people live in places that already are over one hundred thousand in population, and one-third of a billion live in the world's 111 super-metropolises of a million or more people. Within the United States alone there are twenty-three super-metropolises where sixty-five million Americans dwell.

The human tides rising out of countryside and village to join the deluge of new urban children are helping create a great force of the future. Urban immigrants and multiplying city babies are new souls, new muscle, new energy, new brains, new customers, new talent, new vigor for building urban communities of dignity and abundance. They form raw material of the most valuable kind which, combined with the cultural and productive machinery of the metropolis, can greatly advance urban civilization.

Nowhere are urban opportunities greater than here in the United States. Our metropolitan centers hold prodigious concentrations of resources for human growth. Here are well-established school systems, churches, technical institutes, business corporations, great universities, daily newspapers, theaters, symphony orchestras, highly organized local governments, networks of voluntary organizations, health and welfare agencies, and much more.

Here are human-sized living areas, neighborhood communities actual or potential, which can be of great support to man in a metropolis and whose development is the chief concern of this book.

For urban man there is boundless opportunity to live in peace and to develop particular talents of every kind. That so many fail to do so, that so many talents are wasted, that so many families and individuals in the city live isolated from its resources and from each other, that so many are in despair and turmoil is a terrible threat to the urban future. The metropolis is man's most spectacular achievement, just as man is God's supreme creation. Love, as well as bitterness, can flower here. The family can grow and unfold aided by the rich variety of human institutions, or it can atrophy and waste away.

The metropolis is a work of human art, and like every such work strives to capture God, to re-incarnate Him, to present us with another facet of His limitless beauty. Men, some consciously, some unconsciously, reflect God in the good things they make for cities: in the sparkling Chicago lake-front; in the drama of rivers, steel mills, and skyscrapers seen from Pittsburgh's Mount Washington; in the sparkling white houses above San Francisco Bay; in the handsomely kept old streets of New Orleans or Boston; in a thousand places, in quiet blocks of well-cared-for homes.

Through its networks of interrelationships, the metropolis opens to each man endless ways to assist his fellow men by generous use of his talents: the teacher who stays with his declining neighborhood school to help the children of newcomers begin the long road to achievement; the calm housewife who quietly gives extra attention to her harassed neighbor's retarded child; the tired businessman who sacrifices nights at home to raise funds for a new church.

The metropolis provides, also, innumerable chances for man to misuse his skills and exploit his fellows: the clever credit merchant who sucks the bewildered newcomer deeper and deeper into debt; the political leader who gains votes by playing on the racial fears of whites; the delinquent teen-ager who uses an attractive wit and physique to bring other teen-agers into revolt against parents and society.

Depersonalization and degradation exist side-by-side with goodness. Temptations are enormous and of infinite variety. Some men become lost, frustrated and hateful. Others grow, learn to love, and contribute to the building of a good city. The urban place sharpens human feelings and relationships. Its pressures and counterpressures bring out the best and the worst in men. One policeman walks a beat with dedication and care. Another shakes down tavern keepers. One mayor works with patience and integrity. Another schemes and seeks only his own selfish gains. One housewife is friendly, humble, and a joy to her street. Another is a cold snob.

The metropolis is a different animal than the big city of forty years ago. That city held most of the population of an area within one set of governmental boundaries; its department stores and shops had nearly all the trade; near its downtown were most of the factories. The big city monopolized the life of the metropolitan area at that time.

Today the suburbs are mushrooming. Dozens of commercial and industrial subcenters have sprung up all across the metropolis. Much shopping is done in suburban shopping plazas and more and more manufacturing is done in outlying industrial parks. There is a multitude of important governments within a single metropolis. People are spreading out, with central-city populations declining while suburban populations grow. Many of the old towns of the metropolis face the same decline as do the aged sections of the inner city.

Apartheid — separation by race — was a relatively minor factor in the big city of the 1920's. Today as the number of Negroes increases rapidly in the central cities but hardly at all in the suburbs and towns, separation and segregation become a looming problem which pervades the thinking of every street in every neighborhood, spawns tensions, and hangs like a time-bomb over all of metropolis. Suburban schools are receiving considerable attention and money, with their percentage of college-bound children high, while most central-city schools are mediocre, with small numbers going to college. The metropolis is in danger of being split into two hostile pieces, one peopled by the haves, the other by the have-nots. The sword of racial and class apartheid could in time cut metropolitan civilization to ribbons.

Industrial technology, corporate management, status-seeking, the rise of new job centers in the West, Southwest, and South—all have helped to make families highly mobile; family roots are less deep, even though there is plenty of evidence of a yearning for roots.

Perhaps much of the moving within metropolis results from the poor quality of our neighborhoods. They are not yet vigorous contemporary communities capable of winning and holding the loyalty of men.

To unfold as a place good for human life, the metropolis would seem to need many things. A vigorous central core to give it unity and cultural and economic vitality. Plentiful jobs or dignified substitutes. Safe streets. Easy movement from one section to another by car and public transit. High quality of education for children and adults. A decisive and strong government. A variety of people in every section so that there are no more racial or economic ghettos. A social system which supports individuals and families in their working out of tranquil, self-reliant life. And strong living areas that are real neighborhood communities.

The chief generator of the magnetic forces which hold the metropolis together is the central core—downtown and the older sections tied closely to it. Here are centered the communications, commerce, education, arts, finance, government, voluntary organizations, entertainment, and corporation control that gives the metropolis order, purpose, and liveliness. The condition of this core affects the whole urban place. It is the heart pumping life to all parts of the metropolis.

James Marston Fitch, professor of architecture at Columbia University, says of the core: "Such centers are unique. There is no technological substitute for their germinal powers. Personal, face-to-face contact; daily friction and exposure to ideas; continual cross-fertilization from various elements in a given field—these are the essential properties of the center."

Material wealth and richness of ideas combine in the central core to create an indispensable setting. Richness and diversity create a way of life which all can enjoy; the resident, the visitor from afar, the suburbanite who comes into the city to work or to see a medical specialist, attend the opera, or cheer at a ball game. Everyone does not have to live at the core, but all can enjoy it. If the core were to fade, life in the metropolis would sink into mediocrity, precisely because choices would become so limited. Smaller outlying centers lack the depth, richness, and force to replace the central core.

Leland Hazard, one of the nation's outstanding businessmen-philosophers, puts it this way: "There can never be more than a few great art galleries, museums of natural history, theaters, symphonies in any one metropolitan area. The stuff of excellence is limited. Of fine conservatories, old trees, noble churches, and cathedrals, great architecture, gracious parks, comprehensive libraries, original manuscripts, rare books—of all these the central city has the principal supply. Such treasures cannot be duplicated in every shopping center."

Large efforts are under way to strengthen the central core. These are part of a general movement putting human brains and ingenuity to work developing the metropolis as a place good for human life rather than letting it grow as an ugly, chaotic mass.

Improvement efforts in the large urban places of America date back a hundred years or more. In large eastern cities, including Boston and New York, the relation of health to housing was recognized in the 1800's, as disease spread through overcrowded tenements. Local and state health laws were enacted in attempts to improve housing conditions. During the 1920's many cities sought orderly growth by setting up city-planning commissions and passing zoning laws to control the use of land.

Federal efforts blossomed under the beginning of the New Deal in 1933. A bold new philosophy of government initiative to end poverty and human misery gained acceptance then. Government became a major force in housing and urban improvement. The first New Deal programs were carried out under strong federal direction and control, and involved slum clearance and the building of public housing in several cities.

As a strong movement with truly large-scale support, urban development dates back to the end of World War II. We came out of the war conscious of being an urban nation. Rural unemployed had flocked to defense jobs in the cities. Suburbs were beginning to explode. Central-city cores were indispensable but old, ugly, and in need of modernization. And the war effort had so stimulated our productive abilities that we were rich enough to do something big.

The nation's feelings were put into words by the Congress in 1949 with this declaration:

> The Congress hereby declares that the general welfare and security of the Nation and the health and living standards of its people require production and related community development sufficient to remedy the serious housing shortage, the elimination of substandard and other inadequate housing through the clearance of slums and blighted areas, and the realization as soon as possible of the goal of a decent home and a suitable living environment for every American family, thus contributing to the development and redevelopment of communities and to the advancement of the growth, wealth, and security of the Nation.

When Congress backed up its declaration with half a billion dollars to assist local governments, urban renewal came into being.

Urban renewal involves planning by local government, federal financial aid to carry out plans, and then demolition of old buildings, and rebuilding principally by private business. This method has become the most drastic of the development tools used in the metropolis, a detonator and catalyst of great force, capable of removing once immovable barriers. It remains, however, only one of a number of development tools.

By the beginning of 1965 there were almost 1700 urban renewal projects completed or begun under the 1949 program, by approximately seven hundred local governments, large and small. About six hundred other local governments were planning projects.

But there is much more to the movement for urban development than urban renewal. President Kennedy, in obtaining an expanded program from the Congress in 1961, pressed this point, stating:

> Urban renewal programs to date have been too narrow to cope effectively with the basic problems facing older cities. We must do more than concern ourselves with bad housing—we must reshape our cities into effective nerve centers for expanding metropolitan areas. Our efforts must be substantially reoriented from slum clearance and slum prevention into positive programs for economic and social regeneration.

President Johnson has continued this concern with urban development, seeking further enlargement of urban renewal efforts, and initiating the "war on poverty" through passage of the Economic Opportunity Act of 1964. The war on poverty is a massive new human renewal effort. Through programs of employment, education, health, housing, and family unity cities will seek to bring the poor to self-sufficiency. The President considers urban development a key element in leading the American people to become "The Great Society." The commitment of the President to the urban place is strong; that of the Congress is still limited, and will be until it fulfills the President's request for a cabinet position of urban affairs.

Using federal aid, and their own resources, many metropolises have generated large development programs. In Pittsburgh a coordinated effort of government, business, and civic organizations has brought into being the glittering new office towers of the Golden Triangle, cleared the air of smoke, built up the medical center where Dr. Salk discovered his polio vaccine, and promoted other great construction projects including a jet airport, and a civic arena with retractable roof. New Haven, under the leadership of a strong and progressive mayor, has used urban renewal, manpower retraining, and the war on poverty to greatly improve the life of the city. Los Angeles has gone in for vast programs of air-pollution control, expressways, and parking lots.

Whether it is a question of a growth metropolis like Houston, Phoenix, or Los Angeles struggling with problems of water, smog, or clogged roads, or a Pittsburgh, New Haven, or Chicago seeking to shake off obsolescence, the utilization of powerful tools like urban renewal and the war on poverty by dedicated citizens and officials will determine the future of the urban place. Some cities make marked progress, some limp along.

To date it is the central core that has been receiving the lion's share of attention in all these cities. Now, however, urban leaders are beginning to take a wider view, realizing that the condition of neighborhoods is of crucial importance in the development of a metropolis. The education of children in old neighborhoods and new suburbs, the policing of residential streets, the vigor of churches, the motivation of unemployed to take retraining, services for the aged—all of these, urban leaders have come to realize, are as important, possibly more important, than new high-rise buildings and wide expressways.

Urban renewal itself is shifting from downtown to the neighborhoods, and from a tool used primarily for clearing to a tool used primarily for preserving. Partly this change is the result of strong reactions of neighborhood people against demolition and relocation, and partly a clearer vision on the part of city-wide leaders of the high worth of community roots in older neighborhoods, and the value of preserving these communities as supports for the constantly arriving new residents. It is relatively easy in rebuilding a metropolis to become so enthralled with new stadiums and shopping centers as to forget that the principal reason for the existence of a metropolis is to provide a place for men to live, grow, and unfold their talents, a place to build a civilization worthy of creatures made in the Divine Image.

The good metropolis is centered on man, helping him to grow as a human being. Man looks to the metropolis to be something more than an endless mass around a central core. He looks to it to be a network of pieces with order and purpose, forming an urban place of unity and vitality. This book is focused on urban living areas and the struggles to develop them as important pieces of metropolis.

KILROE SEMINARY LIBRARY
HONESDALE, PA.

# Chapter 2

## WHAT IS A NEIGHBORHOOD?

Beyond the central downtown core, and between the expressways, shopping centers, industrial plants, and institutional spires of metropolis lie its living streets. Here are the houses and children, schools and churches, the housewives at work, and the workers at rest.

The living streets crisscross and intertwine; small networks of them are formed by various kinds of barriers and markers, visible and invisible—the physical, economic and social factors that define neighborhoods. These small, separate networks are the localities where the mass of urban men center their lives, even though some may move frequently from one locality to another. Here men seek to knit together their human existence. These are the living areas of metropolis which if nurtured and developed can become neighborhood communities supporting human growth.

Without supporting subcommunities the urban place becomes sterile, even destructive, for men. To know an urban place you must tramp its streets and talk to its people as they relax in doorways, water lawns, drink in bars, tend children, paint porches, and shovel snow. To know something about how the networks of streets and people fit together, ask the question: What neighborhood is this you live in? A rich litany of names will come back.

In Chicago, householders will answer Lawndale, Lincoln Park, Hyde Park-Kenwood, Beverly Hills, Cicero, Oak Park, Skokie, Hazel Crest, and other rooted place-names from all across that great flat metropolitan tangle. In New York: Chelsea, Bloomingdale, Morningside, East Harlem, or one of a hundred others in the canyons of streets. In Los Angeles, the answers will be Burbank, North Hollywood, Brooklyn Heights, Sun Valley, Bel Air, Encino. Compton Eads and Cherokee in St. Louis. Charlestown, Roxbury, Winchester in Boston. Mantua, Germantown in Philadelphia. River Park in South Bend. Dixwell in New Haven. Edgemont in Dayton.

There is the cheerful housewife sweeping the steps of her home on a steep Pittsburgh hillside who will tell you her neighborhood is Fineview and, "it includes everybody who lives on the Fineview trolley line." And the aged Denver man who answers, regretfully, that farther beyond is Aurora, and even further Cherry Hill, but "right here is just the edge of downtown."

For many, as for the man in Denver, some locations are mere residential sections, without real identity as local communities. These locations may lack the commonly used services, facilities, and institutions; or the natural boundaries; or simply the traditions that make a neighborhood. The replies in such sections are often "North of Johnson Street," "off the Boulevard."

In the majority of living areas, however, there is some sense of identification, some feeling of belonging to a particular locality within the sprawling metropolis. Such ties are sometimes historic, going back long years in old city areas. But they seem just as strong, too, in some of the postwar suburbs.

The living areas of metropolis are not the slow-changing, pretty, and peaceful settlements of yesterday, which we Americans tend to idealize and which so many families seem to be seeking in their move outward to the new suburbs. Today's urban living places, whether in the old city or in the far-out open spaces, are places of mobility and movement. There is turmoil, sometimes hidden, sometimes in full view. These living areas reflect the swift changes going on in metropolis, and are shaped by its tragedy and talent.

For many men the living area is the place where they can join movements of protest and political action, efforts of planning and urban renewal, or programs of education and job retraining. Much of the most poignant drama of contemporary life unfolds here. The local high school soars with scholarship awards one year and is shattered by a narcotic scandal the next. Job dislocation touches all streets. Everywhere there is racial apprehension. The living areas that rise above the turmoil to become good neighborhood communities, conducive to human growth, are those with a few citizens who care, and who begin using the resources of metropolis.

For one family the neighborhood may encompass several blocks near downtown with a Skid Row through the middle; for another, a set of gridiron city streets lined with 1920 bungalows; for a third a spread of new ranch houses on curved streets not far from an expressway; and so on through all the variety of metropolis. No matter what the location, if lives of people and institutions are interwoven, if certain essential human needs are served and links to the metropolis provided, then it is a neighborhood community.

An urban section where people live without communication, without organization, with few shops, churches, gas stations, and schools used in common, with each household an isolated unit from which its members range out into the metropolis, with little knowledge or care about what goes on in the surrounding streets — such a section is not a neighborhood community, but a mere residential section.

Today such tools of our times as the large corporation, the expressway, the airplane, and television reduce the role of the living area as the main life-center for some sophisticated adults; but for most people the neighborhood continues to be of primary consequence. When a ten-year-old leaves his home and strolls along the sidewalk, he may be going to school, the corner grocery, the parish church, the ball-field; he is moving about in the subworld where he grows up. With American families averaging one move every five years, he may taste several subworlds before he votes. But one subworld or several, the neighborhood is a place that has much to do with shaping the boy's human character, and developing — or failing to develop — his full potential as a person. It is the local community where most children are educated — formally and informally — and for them the content of the neighborhood is crucial. A rich content means much to their development. An empty content can be tragic and often is.

The Minneapolis Planning Commission in its successful effort to make its city one of the most modern and livable in America, plans according to the following principle: "The foundation of the . . . city is the neighborhood. Here it is that democratic, comprehensive planning begins. Small, local organizations, pursuing the common interests and problems of their areas, exemplify a Minneapolis neighborhood in action. The neighborhood is the immediate center of interest for the housewife and homeowners, most schools, churches, and small businessmen."

Sociologist-planner Herbert J. Gans of the University of Pennsylvania, who has studied neighborhood life in Boston and in several suburban communities, makes this comment on the relation of women to the local community: "Women generally find their female friends nearby, especially if they are mothers and are restricted in their movements. In fact, young mothers must usually be able to find compatible people — and therefore, homogeneous neighbors — within a relatively small radius."

The average man spends a large amount of time around or near his home, painting, repairing, puttering with the lawn, watching TV, visiting with neighbors, ushering at church, drinking on the patio and shopping. This is especially true of homeowners, who have increased to 63 percent of the population, and is particularly true of suburban homeowners, who are growing at the fastest rate. Another sociologist who has studied the modern metropolis is Scott Greer. In his fascinating book, *The Emerging City,* he states:

> Though the suburban neighborhood is not the site of the husband's occupation, he spends most of his free time there — 60 or 70 hours each week. And, for his wife and children, the residential neighborhood is the center of the world. The bedroom community is, in many matters, the basic community.

To be sure there are now "metropolitan men" — mobile, worldly-wise, able to comprehend the whole vast urban complex — for whom the metropolis itself is the local community. They are a small, growing breed usually with connections to one or more metropolises in addition to their home base. But like the elite of any society they are few in number, and probably will be for a long time.

In spite of mobility, population sprawl, redevelopment, high-rise construction, and dire predictions, the fabric of neighborhood has not been disappearing. But it has been undergoing profound change. Whole new kinds of suburban neighborhoods have been springing up overnight. In the crowded central cities — traditional wellsprings of culture and new ideas — a majority of neighborhoods have been caught in the enveloping gray zone of blight, with a chosen few starting down the long urban renewal road toward ordered rearrangement.

The role of the neighborhood in American society is not a mere academic matter. The future influence — or lack of influence — of the neighborhood will partly determine the form and role of institutions, including church and school as well as the family. And it will certainly have a profound effect on the nation's massive development and antipoverty programs now beginning to restyle and restore metropolitan areas. We can have neighborhoods, and good ones, if we work for them.

At stake is the nature of urban life itself. Is there to be local community life, or only the big, impersonal mass of metropolis? This is no emotional question asked only by soft-headed idealists. It is also a concern of the hard-headed who deal with the city in financial terms. A mortgage banker like James E. Rouse, who has promoted some of the country's largest postwar shopping centers, speaks as follows about the metropolis: "The big job is to break it up into human-being sized neighborhoods in which people can live and shop, go to church, play and raise families. We must create neighborhoods that are human in scale, in which families can feel a sense of belonging, about the care and maintenance of which they can feel concerned, and in which they can take a healthy pride."

It is even possible that the significance of the neighborhood to people increases as the metropolis expands in size and intricacy. Man's height is little changed from that of the rural man of one hundred years ago; his eyes see no farther; his mind works no faster. Unlike the computer, his memory cannot hold and accurately draw forth millions of identifications. In spite of his modern props and apparatus, he is in some ways the same limited rural man in a vastly more complicated environment.

The average person has need for a place of limited

scale where he not only establishes a home but from which he can face the enormity of the metropolis. The neighborhood has long been a basic ingredient of American life. It was when the first American settlements were built in Massachusetts and Virginia. It was when towns were founded and flourished across the nation. It remained so as towns became cities, for cities have grown largely as clusters of neighborhoods around the downtown central core.

Jean Gottmann, the French geographer, in his deep and detailed studies of the huge urbanized northeastern seaboard of the United States (a complex of several metropolises he calls "megalopolis") notes the strong tendency of Americans to partition themselves into "a mosaic of small communities." Gottmann traces the American roots of this tendency back to the New England self-governing township, the self-contained Southern plantation, and the early communities established by religious sects and ethnic groups.

The history of urban neighborhoods is a long one. The contemporary neighborhood is more than a survival from rural and small-town America. In part, its roots go back to the cities of Europe, and to the Mediterranean world of antiquity.

Ancient Rome had districts, many with their own temple, public bathhouse, and market, around which a local community life was centered. The urban neighborhood as a livable place with a sense of unity flowered in the Middle Ages. In *The City in History,* Lewis Mumford describes the medieval neighborhood thus:

> The division of the town into quarters, each with its church or churches, often with a local provision market, always with its own local water supply, a well or a fountain, was a characteristic feature; but as the town grew the quarters might become sixths, or even smaller fractions of the whole, without dissolving into

the mass. Often, as in Venice, the neighborhood unit would be identified with the parish and get its name from the parish church: a division that remains to this day.

The independence of the medieval city, its neighborhoods, and citizens, declined after the fourteenth century with the rise of the absolute state. The Reformation destroyed much neighborhood cohesiveness along with religious unity. Most of the physical delight of the medieval neighborhood was obliterated by the soot of industrialism and the exploitation of laissez-faire capitalism, which glorified long working hours, low pay, and maximum economic return from real estate — maximum return meaning overcrowding and ugliness.

American cities grew up during the age of industrialism. From their earliest days many were bleak, congested places. But they had in them a local community life brought by immigrants from European cities and villages, and by rural Americans coming to work in the city. The industrial quarters into which they moved developed as neighborhoods, some with specific names and identities (Bridgeport and Pullman in Chicago; Hazelwood and Manchester in Pittsburgh; Harlem Park in Baltimore, and so on).

Modern city-planning was born out of reaction to the exploitation common to industrial living. One of the fathers of the ideas that dominate planning today was Ebenezer Howard, a London clerk who revolted against the fearful crowding of late nineteenth-century London families into airless and sunless slums. His solution was self-contained garden towns in the countryside around London. Each town was to be carefully planned, with separate areas for stores, homes, factories, and recreation, all set amidst profuse grass and trees. Population in each town was to be limited to about twenty-five or thirty thousand.

In 1920 an American planner, Clarence Perry, refined the Howard idea into a small self-contained city neighborhood, with definite boundaries, and a population limited to that sufficient to support an elementary school. This self-contained neighborhood was to have the same rigid division of land uses, centralized shopping and playground compound, and the quiet residential streets of Ebenezer Howard's plan.

The Howard-Perry concept dominated nearly all neighborhood planning of the last generation. Attractive, successful use of the concept can be seen in Riverside, Illinois; Baldwin Hills, California; Radburn, New Jersey; and Chatham Village, Pittsburgh. The ideas of these men are reflected in nearly all the planned postwar suburbs and the greenswards and malls of urban renewal projects. Of these later adaptations in suburbs and urban renewal projects, some are not successful, being monotonous, stereotyped, and not always fitting the needs of the people and localities they are meant to serve.

Opposition to the neighborhood concept in planning arose after World War II when urban renewal was beginning to grow as a movement of force. Leading the attack was Reginald Isaacs, then a Chicago planner, now a Harvard professor, who viewed neighborhood planning as a fruitless attempt to make static residential areas in the midst of mobile and dynamic cities; and worse — as an instrument of racial, ethnic, social, and economic segregation. A number of distinguished planners, architects, and social scientists lined up on Isaacs' side of this controversy. But the antineighborhood position has never won wide acceptance among planners, in part because they have never found a satisfactory alternative to it.

In 1954, the federal government laid down special requirements a city must meet before receiving urban renewal grants; one of these is neighborhood planning. In the early sixties, the American Society of Planning

Officials reviewed the whole question, and reported: "Judging from the great number of existing plans still hewing closely to Perry's original [neighborhood] concept . . . it appears that much of the momentum of the opposition movement has been exhausted." Today one finds most new suburban areas being planned along the Howard-Perry lines. The same process can be seen being utilized in the renewal of old-city neighborhoods.

When planners, renewal operators, and other officials begin to move actively against concrete problems of deteriorating housing, overcrowding, and all the rest, they find they can only take hold of a small piece of the city at a time. Their funds and manpower are limited, the number of families they can relocate is relatively few and they can only deal with small property owners at the level of the neighborhood. What they are doing is attempting to find ways for urban man's basic physical and social needs to be well served. This inevitably requires some kind of decentralization of services.

Officials usually find in any area some general neighborhood boundaries on which citizens can agree, boundaries that enclose a district which citizens can identify, often with a specific neighborhood name. Planning and executing of renewal projects on this local area basis is tending to deepen neighborhood identification. The renewal project adopts and publicizes the neighborhood name. It gives the people of the area opportunity for participation in a common endeavor of immense personal concern, whether this concern takes the form of support or opposition to the project.

The same need for a small, cohesive geographic area in which to come to grips with problems exists for many planners and operators in social renewal. We find youth commissions, health and welfare associations, the new war-on-poverty organizations, even psychiatric projects organizing programs at a neighborhood level. There seems, however, to be an uneasy feeling among planners, urban renewal operators, neighborhood workers, social scientists, and others that the issue is not resolved. They see the ease with which people move, frequently and far; the wide variety of communities in which many people spend their lives; the boredom of some of their friends in planned suburbs; the lack of place identity in some sections of metropolis. They see that many people now satisfy some needs once met in the neighborhood, through communities formed by their co-workers in job or profession, or through those with whom they share a common cultural interest. Modern man does form such communities but they are often temporary and without substance. They seldom connect a man with the metropolis beyond.

Some social scientists who study American life see the neighborhood as a dying community. Two examples of these are Emile Pin, who has looked at the local church in American urban life, and Roland L. Warren, who in 1963 published his provocative book, *The Community in America*. Pin, in *Apostolate* magazine, declared that: ". . . in the modern large city the unit of residence is no longer a local community. . . . The streams of life do not any longer pass through the locality groupings . . . the common theatre of all the activities of the closest neighbors is not their residence unit but the whole city. The neighborhood community . . . has been emptied of most of its content and there is no doubt that it will not regain it."

Warren, in his book, raises skepticism as to whether the neighborhood is any longer significant. He sees the local neighborhood community as one of the victims of what he terms the "great change" in American community living:

. . . the great change in community living includes the

increasing orientation of local community units to state and national systems. . . . Decisions, policies, and programs of local units, although they must conform in some respects to community norms, come to be formulated in centralized offices outside the community and come to be guided more by their relation to extra-community systems than by their relation to other parts of the local community. Thus the ties between different local community units are weakened, and community autonomy, defined as control by local people over the establishment, goals, policies, and operation of local community units, is likewise reduced.

By this Warren would seem to mean that the neighborhood church now is more concerned with its ties to the downtown denominational headquarters than to the local community in which it is located. The neighborhood supermarket is more closely related to its remote central office than to the neighborhood community. The school principal's eyes and ears are more keenly attuned to the superintendent's office than to the neighborhood in which his school is located. These links, however, are a strength as well as a weakness. They feed back to the neighborhood resources it needs to service its residents. The traditional self-contained neighborhood of earlier times had fewer such links and was not able to serve its residents as well. Strong links to the resources of the metropolis, and the nation beyond, are an important element for the modern neighborhood and one that keeps it relevant.

The change Pin and Warren observe is the neighborhood becoming less the major focal point of urban living, and more just one of several focal points. This change alters some of the neighborhood's functions, but it does not destroy its usefulness to man. It means the contemporary neighborhood is only one of urban man's supporting communities; although it has dropped some of its past functions, it has also taken on new ones.

A study of a large neighborhood in northwest St.

Louis, for instance, done by Sociologist Donald L. Foley shortly after World War II, revealed sharp contrasts in those services residents obtained within their local community, and those obtained outside it; he found a surprising amount of services still obtained inside the neighborhood. Sporting events, medical services, new clothes and furniture, and employment were sought outside the neighborhood, while an overwhelming amount of the food-shopping, school and church attendance was done in and around the neighborhood. Concluded Foley, "Our large cities, for all their urbanity, seem to contain an impressive degree of local community life within metropolitan limits."

The neighborhood community is changing, and like the metropolis itself is becoming more complex. The successful modern urban neighborhood must be something different — something contemporary, part of its time. It is now only one of several geographic communities, all of which play an important role in the metropolis and none of which are self-sufficient.

This community-within-communities concept is explored in Jane Jacobs' *The Death and Life of Great American Cities*. Her book contains a scathing attack on the Howard-Perry concepts of quiet streets and rigid zoning, but makes a strong case for the preservation of lively urban neighborhoods, especially old ones. With impressive logic, Mrs. Jacobs points out that there are really three communities in a city: the street area right where people live; the district neighborhood with which people identify and which is big enough to get what its people need from city hall; and the metropolis itself.

Social scientist Greer, in *The Emerging City,* sees similar levels of community. He begins with the family (he finds kinship relations to be of more importance than ever in urban society); moves to the immediate area of across-the-fence friendships and visiting patterns; then to the local neighborhood district where the voluntary organizations, ward politics, and community newspapers operate; and finally to the metropolis itself. This analysis agrees with the experience of many community organization workers who struggle with the remaking of the city as their profession. They, too, find that the neighborhood of significance for local community action is the district neighborhood.

Floyd Agostinelli, an energetic and dedicated neighborhood worker in Washington, D.C., says of his own experience:

> If one starts from an old concept of neighborhood — one whose geography is restricted to two or three blocks — then a neighborhood concept seems utterly inadequate as an instrumentality in meeting the problems of the city. It is inadequate because within this restricted geographic limitation, there is not enough intrinsic talent and wherewithal to make a positive contribution to city life.
>
> However, with a larger neighborhood concept the reverse is true. There is the intrinsic wherewithal to make a positive contribution. In Washington, D.C., we have neighborhoods such as Woodridge, Ivy City, Anacostia, Marshall Heights, Georgetown, Cleveland Park. These neighborhoods contain very sizable populations and contain many "old time" neighborhoods. It is this new neighborhood, with its rather sizable population that gives an individual an instrumentality that he can personally identify with, and secondly, gives him an instrumentality that can readily be an object of a planning or improvement program.
>
> The present-day community has this unique quality: it can bring together for a common purpose persons who have no common objective other than the neighborhood objective.

The district neighborhood corresponds roughly to Ebenezer Howard's concept of a town large enough for its own shopping center, to Jane Jacobs' district big enough to swing political weight, and to Greer's area that is large enough to support community organizations. The size of such districts will vary depending upon the size of the metropolis.

It is district neighborhoods like Chicago's Hyde Park-Kenwood, Pittsburgh's Homewood-Brushton, Boston's Charlestown, San Francisco's Buena Vista, New York's Greenwich Village that have emerged as important local urban communities. They not only have the strength that comes from having their own identity, but the unity conferred by central shopping, common schools, churches, and recreational facilities. They are large enough to be effective service districts. They have sufficient leadership and political force to undertake the joint action that helps create a community. They are important enough to receive recognition from the whole metropolis and so to be a link to it. Generally the district neighborhood contains from ten thousand to fifty thousand people, and ranges from one-half to three square miles in area. In a large metropolis, like Chicago or New York City, these figures may be greater; in a smaller place, like Raleigh or San Diego, they may be less. This size is usually a logical one for planning and renewal programs.

To feel the warmth and intensity of identity in a district neighborhood, travel to Pittsburgh's Hazelwood-Glenwood. Talk to any of the citizens and you will hear them speak affectionately and unself-consciously of their neighborhood as "the town." You will find most shop on the same two blocks on Second Avenue, more than half belong to the same parish church, and hundreds work in a neighborhood organization, the Hazelwood-Glenwood Urban Extension Council.

People in a district neighborhood have roots in it and a loyalty to it. They are usually ready to participate in the rebuilding of the city by working to revitalize their own "town." Without the energies of people in such neighborhoods, the metropolis can never be a good living environment. Government alone does not have the time, money, or know-how to do the whole job of urban development. Nor would it be good for the nation if government could do this job alone, for it is from participation, the citizen taking on responsibility, that some of the deepest psychological needs of men are served and sense of community developed. Throughout this book, the word neighborhood refers to the large district neighborhood.

New York City, as the nation's largest and most complex metropolis, is a primary place to test whether the neighborhood community serves any of the needs of modern man. It is probably the noisiest, dirtiest, most crowded, exciting, and wealthy urban place in the world. What its people and officials think and do about neighborhoods is significant. The New York Regional Plan Association has had a selected sample of several thousand New Yorkers watch five television programs about the future of their metropolis. After each television program, participants discussed urban issues in small groups, and then filled out individual questionnaires.

Revealed were strong feelings that city neighborhoods should be strengthened in relation to city government. Three-quarters said it is very important to provide channels of communication between neighborhood groups and city government. More than half felt it was very important to have subcenters of government in different parts of the city to provide information on the city's programs; about as many felt it was very important to have sectional school boards able to make some decisions within the over-all policy of the city-wide school board.

Harry C. Harris, who for several years was staff director for New York's City's sizable neighborhood conservation program, and who is now deeply involved in the city's war-on-poverty effort, believes governmental services are best administered on a neighborhood basis.

Partly through his leadership "neighborhood city halls" were established in twenty-two New York living areas, and the number continues to increase under his successor. Harris points out that the average city household once kept close to government through the ward political leader who was an active and important neighborhood person. Today the local political leader's influence is gone and he plays little part in dispensing services. The ward leader was replaced in the thirties and forties by highly centralized, professional city government. This was government with engineers and public administrators overseeing services. It has been efficient, but bureaucratic. And as with all bureaucracies, it has tended to become rigid and far away from the people, and in many respects no longer serves their needs. With the neighborhood city hall and neighborhood citizens' organization linking the citizen to local government, such government is made more vital, less bureaucratic, and better services local needs.

New York City has also been experimenting with district planning boards. The city's five boroughs have been divided into a number of districts each of which is to have a citizens' planning board appointed by the Borough President, under a new city charter which takes full effect in 1968. The districts follow traditional neighborhood lines, such as Harlem, Flatbush, Jamaica, Fordham, and St. George. Each board will advise the Borough President, the City Planning Commission and the Borough Improvement Board, on neighborhood needs. The citizens' planning boards will be consulted on housing, social services, welfare, hospitals and health, schools, parks and recreation centers, libraries, civic defense and other matters. Chicago has legally constituted Community Conservation Councils, appointed by the mayor for each neighborhood urban renewal area where major emphasis is on rehabilitating homes rather than tearing them down. These are citizens' councils of eleven to fifteen members with actual legal power over the content of the plan for their neighborhood.

John E. Hirtin, who is director of San Francisco's citizen planning and urban renewal association, feels neighborhoods should have an even more direct link to city government. Hirtin believes that if the neighborhood is to strengthen its identity and political importance, it must have some kind of official representation. The traditional ward system in many cities provided local representation to the city council, but this system no longer works well because city problems are so large and complex that councilmen with a city-wide responsibility are needed. Also, ward lines often cut through neighborhoods. The neighborhood city hall method in New York City probably best answers the need that Hirtin expresses, or perhaps it would be even better answered by a strong full-time professional representative employed by the neighborhood to keep open the lines to city hall. Such professionals will be discussed in Chapter 8, and a picture of one at work will be found in Chapter 9.

These efforts in New York, Chicago, San Francisco — and similar efforts elsewhere — are simply attempts to humanize the metropolis by strengthening and modernizing neighborhoods. There would seem to be four major elements an urban living area needs before it becomes a neighborhood, relevant and useful to modern man:

1. Adequate facilities and services to meet certain immediate human needs:

— attractive, well-maintained housing, selling and renting at fair prices;
— handy and pleasant supermarkets, laundromats, bars, parks, and playgrounds designed and run to serve

the particular needs of local people, and set up in such a way as to provide communications among people;

— vital church congregations of local people with clergymen and lay leaders active in the life of the neighborhood;

— excellent schools able to draw out fully the talents of neighborhood children;

— well-run public services, including police and fire protection, water, sewerage, garbage collection, street sweeping and lighting, that help bring order and cleanliness.

2. Forces that build a sense of community:

— an interesting community newspaper through which people debate local issues and share knowledge of local events and of each other;

— neighborhood political and civic organizations through which people can plan and act for themselves and utilize fully the assets of their own community and the vast resources of the whole metropolis;

— responsible families who promote the use and growth of neighborhood resources, have local pride and identity.

3. Links to the whole metropolis:

— accessibility by streets, expressways, and fast public transit to other parts of the metropolis;

— working relationships between neighborhood leaders and government and other metropolitan resources;

— a wide outlook and sense of responsibility toward the whole metropolis by neighborhood leaders.

4. Some mixture and integration of all kinds of people of metropolis:

— acceptance of new neighbors on their merits;

— an awareness of the special importance in our time of racial equality and a willingness to live it.

These are the criteria for a strong and modern neighborhood. Probably no neighborhood anywhere has yet achieved them all. There are many living areas working toward achieving them. In later chapters some neighborhoods in which local people are making outstanding efforts to build vigorous neighborhood life will be examined in depth. It is well to keep in mind that in all neighborhood development efforts there is special danger and special opportunity. The danger is narrow localism, a provincialism which fastens a householder's sights wholly on his own neighborhood to the exclusion of the outside world. The opportunity is human growth. It comes with vision, the gaining of a broad understanding of the needs of both the living streets of a neighborhood and of the whole metropolis.

# Chapter 3

## PIECES OF METROPOLIS

Each living area of metropolis is a neighborhood community in being or in potential. Many are fine service districts, and some have effective linkage to the whole metropolis, but most have their sense of community in cold storage. Only a handful have stable racial integration.

No two living areas are exactly alike, but most seem to fall into one of six types. We gain a better understanding of what it takes to make strong neighborhood communities by giving consideration to these different types. Three types are to be found in the central-city core, and three in the great settled spaces beyond. The central core living areas are:

> Slums
> Gray Areas
> Redevelopment Areas

Three outlying types are:

> Postwar Tract Suburbs
> Plush Suburban Villages
> Old Towns

*The Slums*

The slum is a piece of metropolis in chaos. It does badly as a service district; there are pockets in it with a sense of community, but little of this quality over-all; links to the wider urban place are ineffective, with most of the rest of the metropolis anxious to ignore and forget the slum's existence.

Slums are the old areas of cities filled with the poor and the newcomers, some of whom are on the way up, some mired in the slum hopelessly. Streets and buildings are old, obsolete, and neglected. There is exploitation by credit merchants, landlords, vice operators. There is a great welfare network which struggles ineffectually to insure some minimum decent existence for the poorest. There is often a chronic threat of destruction of homes by planned public projects. And there are deep-seated frustrations provoking violence. There are churches which like the welfare institutions give solace but, with few exceptions, do little to stir people to break their bonds of poverty.

In the past the schools have been largely indifferent to conditions in the slum, thus contributing to the present apathy and deprivation there. Those who came to the schools ready to learn, anxious to improve themselves, were helped; but vast numbers of children, unmotivated and with undeveloped talents, were given little inspiration. Now this is changing, and the schools of the slums are becoming centers of experimentation and innovation. With grants from foundations and the government, crash programs are being pushed by a new breed of post-war educators who see inner city education as an exciting and significant mission.

Most urban slums today are Negro ghettos or are fast becoming ghettos. And within these areas revolutionary fever is spreading, bursting out in rent strikes, protest marches, juvenile lawlessness, and full-scale riots. In those cities where the ghettos are rapidly expanding there is political power within reach of the new militant, revolutionary leadership. The stage is set for increased conflict.

Slums in which there are leaders of initiative and people of hope are quite different from those dominated by despair. Slums of hope are dominated by poor people of some ability who are confident they can better themselves. They may be newcomers who need only to learn the language and ways of operating in the city; or Negroes of ability who need only to break across the discrimination barrier. Slums of despair are occupied largely by people who lack ability, confidence, or both. All slums have both kinds of people. This distinction is an important one when considering how to approach physical and human renewal within slums. This distinction has been convincingly analyzed by Charles J. Stokes, writing in *Land Economics*.

Stokes cites Chicago's Negro South Side, Bronzeville, as a slum of hope. Here are aggressive people, establishing their own newspapers, magazines, insurance companies, factories, shops. They are building their own city, and pushing toward increased political power. Stokes says of such residents: "Evidencing above average mental and social talents, as they acquire a permanent foothold in the city into which they have come, they are more likely to reclaim their neighborhoods, if they can (as in Baltimore) or if they can't they will push toward better neighborhoods."

As an example of a neighborhood dominated by despair, Stokes points to Boston's South End, an area of once-fine homes and still fine trees, pervaded by decay. Here lives the social residue; old, poor, cast-off Bostonians; immigrants unable to learn successfully the ways of the city; and shady characters, prostitutes and small-time gamblers.

Says Stokes:

> The barriers to movement upward and outward for the South Ender are largely subjective. The poverty one sees in its streets appears to have some correlation with the large number of taverns. The South End does not expand physically. It slowly dies and with it what was once one of the best areas in Boston.

These are those for whom society has pity but has somehow been unable to help effectively. It is unlikely that the major part of the inhabitants of the slums of "despair" will ever leave them but there does appear to be a steady movement into them.

In slums where hope dominates the major challenge is to furnish the hopeful with the opportunities and resources to peacefully and radically change their world. In a slum dominated by despair, the critical question is whether despair can be changed to hope and slum conditions removed. A great effort is now being made to do this in Boston's South End, with citizen groups organized through the South End settlements and massive assistance being provided through the Boston Redevelopment Authority, the city's public urban renewal agency, and through Action for Boston Community Development, a private nonprofit human renewal agency. This effort may improve the South End as a service district, but a sense of community will depend on response from the people who live or work in the South End.

Deep-down renewal of a slum, beyond mere surface physical change, depends in large part on the kind of leadership that can rise up out of the slums themselves. One of the most effective neighborhood leaders in Pittsburgh is a man of hope named Clyde Battles who lives in the city's Hill District slum. With a wife, four children, and a couple of relatives he rents a decaying five-room row-house, which he is constantly repairing. Around him live households with husbandless mothers and old people on public assistance who turn to Battles when rats become too numerous, when they need an emergency drive to the hospital, or for advice on whether redevelopment is coming. Battles does maintenance work on and off for the slumlord who owns his house. He is held back in life by a medical history of epilepsy, limited education, and his color.

Shared desperation, common hatred of landlords and concern for children, and Battles' leadership, has given his block some sense of community and even links to downtown, but his area of influence is yet too small to demand and get the services his people need. Month after month, year after year he pushes ahead — trying, organizing, learning, finding allies; one day soon he may help cause revolt and renewal within the whole Hill area. (And as new kinds of human renewal programs grow and take on subprofessional staff members of ability, Battles may finally find himself with a career. And perhaps then he will lose some of his effectiveness.)

To make possible changes in the lives of the despairing, and to open opportunities to the hopeful, is immensely complicated. How do we build neighborhoods where the poor, the alcoholic, the broken can live in some peace amid surroundings that have some dignity? Where are the supports and facilities to drain despair from those capable of hope? How do we open the mainstream of society to those with ability? How do we recognize and bring forth leadership within the slums and enlist the support of those outside the slums? Physical changes are essential in slums. The removal of rotting housing, abandoned factories, broken streets, along with building anew, will help restore hope along with health and economic strength.

Employment, safe streets, education, self-respect — these social changes are even more vital. The most difficult part of the transformation of slums is going to be the thawing out of the ghetto glacier and the accomplishment of racial integration where today there is none. The will to do this does not yet seem to exist among political leaders or neighborhood people, white or Negro. The knowledge of how to plan and achieve it is only dimly perceived.

More and more those in positions of responsibility —

mayors, planners, neighborhood leaders — are coming to
believe there should be a leisurely rebuilding of the physical slum and a crash rebuilding of the social slum. Urban
renewal can provide most of the resources for physical
rebuilding. The government's war on poverty offers the
resources for social rebuilding. It is up to urban leadership, citizen and professional, to put the resources to
work.

The Negro protest movement now growing in most
slums is probably the force which will not only compel
the metropolis to establish links with the slum and give
it the services it needs, but also will build a sense of solidarity and community within the slum.

## The Gray Areas

Most numerous of the central city residential sections
are the gray areas. These are the aging, declining, but
still sound living areas which cover much of the land in
every central city. They are once-pleasant areas on their
way to becoming slums. Luther Gulick, the dean of public administrators, has called them "massed areas of con-
tiguous obsolescence." Gray areas, over-all, are undis-
tinguished and ugly, but pockets within them are still
quite attractive. Most have names, and a degree of identity, and many are genuine neighborhoods with cohesion and a network of services and relationships. They
have problems, but not yet the crisis and degradation of
the slums. In these areas, police protection, street maintenance, and other governmental services have been deteriorating along with houses and stores. Parents worry
that their children will drop out of school, or be attacked
by gangs. Worse, they may fear their children will join
a gang and be caught slashing tires, stealing cars, or
using narcotics. Movement of whites out and Negroes in
has been taking place at a pace that is making new
ghettos.

The gray areas of America contain huge quantities of solid buildings and millions of families. Their populations, however, are decreasing as families move to the suburbs. From the gray areas of the older cities of the East and Midwest there is also migration of single adults and young families to the cities of the West and Southwest in search of jobs and low-cost higher education.

Since the exodus out of gray areas is greater than the movement of newcomers in, elbow room for renewal efforts is enlarged.

Gray areas can be assets for a city but require enormous effort from citizens to improve their own property and from local government to improve public facilities — a common effort of citizens and government for replanning, rebuilding, and reinvigorating that will lift morale, and create a vision of the vital communities gray areas can become in the modern metropolis.

No gray area is standing still. The way of the metropolis is change. Every gray area is either declining or growing. Most are in decline. The few that are growing are not increasing in population or in size, but are growing in spirit, with new or modernized buildings replacing old, and public services being strengthened. These are the relatively few where there are active development efforts. Most people in gray areas have incomes in the $3000 to $8000 range, although there are those who earn more and some who are poverty stricken. The stable people who remain are older and the newcomers are largely young and poor.

These areas can serve vital purposes in the city as living places for families of limited means, as a home-base for newcomers, and as a haven for middle-income people who like the vitality and convenience of the central city. The closer a gray area comes to being a strong neighborhood community the more perfectly it can fulfill these purposes.

There are two kinds of gray areas that deserve special mention. One of these is the old ethnic neighborhood, the other is the area of faded elegance. The old ethnic neighborhood is one of white immigrants and their descendants — Poles, Irish, Italians, Eastern Europeans — most of whom came here some years ago. These neighborhoods are remnants of the past. They are old style areas; villages in the city. There remains some sense of community centered around interconnected families, nationality clubs, and churches. The Italian neighborhood has its Italian store, the Irish neighborhood its Irish bar, the German neighborhood its Turners Hall, and in all there is a common fear of the approach of Negroes. The ethnic neighborhood often maintains links to metropolis through its bloc voting and ties to the Democratic Party.

If somehow the ethnic neighborhood could lose its narrowness, particularly its racial hostility, and build on its great strengths, it could probably regain vitality and make a substantial contribution to the modern metropolis. Its strengths are real. The distinctive flavor of a foreign culture is enriching and adds to the diversity of the metropolis. The pride in these areas, reflected in neat, well-cared-for homes is immense. But such neighborhoods are dying out, as the young marry and move quickly away seeking bright suburbs and full Americanization. There is not the new housing or community vigor to hold them.

Pittsburgh's South Side is typical of many such areas. Narrow, picturesque streets lined with small, old, brightly painted houses, display windows ashine, polished aluminum storm doors, cement steps washed down; but the area is losing population faster than the rest of the city. Knock on doors along a South Side block and you find eight out of ten householders are in their fifties or older. The South Side has great charm and a splendid location, yet is slipping away. Great forces from within and from without the area would have to be generated and joined together to save the assets of the South Side, and to begin to transform it into a strong urban neighborhood.

Lawrence Ragan is a college professor and editor of Chicago's thoughtful little magazine, *New City*. He is a suburban father and husband who grew up in a central-city ethnic neighborhood. In this sketch from his magazine he looks back at his old Irish neighborhood:

In the lives of many who grow up in big cities there is only one "neighborhood." Ours was that mile or so that radiates from St. Gabriel's parish at 45th and Lowe. Sometimes its inhabitants referred to it as Canaryville, although it is not a name widely used outside its environs.

Like all neighborhoods, ours has changed and is changing with the years. I knew a different Canaryville in the late forties than did Upton Sinclair when at the turn of the century he wrote about parts of it in *The Jungle*. And, today, change continues to make itself felt. As my friend put it, "Nobody lives in the old neighborhood any more."

He was wrong, of course; many people still live in Canaryville. Many of them have lived there all their lives. Husbands often have met their wives for the first time as they played together in sandboxes. True, the Canaryville expatriate and his descendants populate vast areas of Chicago's Southside and whenever Irishmen meet and ask about the old neighborhood, at least one of them surely is referring to those few blocks sandwiched between Halsted and the tracks, just east of the Yards.

Some Canaryville natives leave to establish a home elsewhere, then decide they must return. They weren't happy on alien soil, where the beer wasn't as cold, the neighbors weren't as friendly, the church wasn't as cheerful as St. Gabe's with its angels perched aloft with electric lights held in their upraised hands.

Unlike some neighborhoods, Canaryville has no dreams of glory or splendor to look back upon. Today it is considerably quieter and more comfortable than it was a generation or two ago. But improved conditions are not a substitute for memories of the past, which are mostly of people. Like my wife's grandfather who was pushed in a wheelbarrow, the story is told, from the Chicago fire to 45th and Wallace, the site of his new home, where today his great-great-grandchildren continue to live. Older residents of Canaryville have no difficulty in recalling Father Burke, St. Gabriel's second pastor, who imported marble from Italy to re-do the altar. That meant a quarter-at-the-door and a dime-in-the-box, which outrage drove more than one parishioner to neighboring St. Cecilia.

Canaryville is a neighborhood where nicknames flourish, where Potato Head Pat Murphy and Carburetor Mike Gilhooley and Roary-up-the-Hill — no, not Roaring but Roary — Mulligan spent many a quiet summer's evening in front of McInerney's, the funeral home from which Father Dorney, the parish's first pastor, was buried, and on whose wall still is displayed the list of mourners who were part of the funeral procession. They are a sentimental people, Potato Head Pat and Carburetor Mike, especially on such occasions as Mother's Day, when the men of the parish march to eight o'clock Mass down the middle of the streets, converging upon the church from three different directions, each group being led by a brass band. It is not a quiet time for those who enjoy sleeping late on a Sunday morning.

Whenever I hear of the conformity said to exist in the suburbs I think of Canaryville. One could be little else but a conformist when one's world was bounded by the Yards, the corner saloon, perhaps, where (as my mother-in-law would put it) the "bottle gang" hung out, and the home on whose front steps one called out to the neighbors on the front steps next door and across the street. I have heard it alleged that there are those in the neighborhood who would lose their way if by some mischance fate took them south of 55th Street or north of Root.

Such statements, of course, are exaggerations and maybe never had any truth in them. In the late forties, when I knew Canaryville, the war was over and the young men had returned, bringing with them strange tales of a non-Irish world. And pretty Canaryville girls found jobs in the Loop as well as in the Yards. They on occasion brought home, heaven help us, non-Irish boyfriends.

Still, thinking of Canaryville, one tends to think according to the stereotypes because it so perfectly fulfills the idea of what may be a vanishing city phenomenon. Canaryville was and is a neighborhood in a way unknown to Hyde Park and South Shore and Marquette Park. It was and is provincial and narrow-minded, but withal a wonderful and exciting place. It is, after all, the old neighborhood. I wonder if my children in later years shall respond in the same way to their neighborhood.

One sees in Ragan's nostalgic sketch the emphasis on the parish church as the central institution, giving identity and cohesion to the Canaryville neighborhood, and on the street characters who gave vitality and personality. The sense of community came in large part from ethnic unity. In the ethnic gray areas today this unity is breaking up, and with its disappearance comes the opportunity for such neighborhoods to widen their horizons, lose their narrowness, contribute more of the richness of their community to the whole metropolis, establish stronger links, and draw increased strength from its diversity.

Such neighborhoods need modernization of their services, and a citizens' joint effort to achieve such modernization could perhaps be the new source of sense of community.

Neighborhoods of this kind offer good living opportunities for families of modest income. Among their features are: small, economical remodelled houses; con-

venience to job and to the services and culture of the
central core; familiar, fully developed institutions at
hand. These are assets on which to build a neighborhood
of considerable attraction. Not mentioned by Ragan are
the strains of racial tension which surround Canaryville
and nearly every other gray area in large old cities; nor
does he speak of the dirt, bleakness, and crime. These,
however, are physical problems which can be conquered.
He is most concerned with warmth and lack of sham,
qualities perhaps more difficult to find in the suburb to
which he has migrated.

One of the largest barriers to modernization of gray
areas, particularly the ethnic gray area, is the inflexi-
bility and obsolescence of many of its traditional organizations and institutions. Their continued existence gives
a false sense of well-being. Their policy is to resist change.
A neighborhood worker of considerable perception gives
this analysis of his own area:

> Everyone is attached to an ethnic-group church,
> social club, or affiliate. This seems to be the status
> symbol for the white lower middle-class. At one time
> these groups served a purpose; reference points for
> immigrants, fund raisers, minor services, and the like.
>
> From them sprang the local Chamber of Commerce
> which was supposed to agitate for larger community
> services. It has been largely unsuccessful, however,
> and so has only attracted those who had no other
> home.
>
> In a sense it only succeeded in creating another
> clique. The Chamber in the neighborhood long repre-
> sented the self-appointed "community leadership." But
> the real power elite in the neighborhood, those who
> control the resources and funds, is comprised of many
> clans.
>
> These have no vision of planning, modern services,
> or expansion. Their way of doing business belongs

strictly to the old order, which has failed utterly to attract any new blood, especially young adults.

The power structure of the neighborhood, collectively, is representative of the community but its members never really associate with each other. They leave the neighborhood fragmented. They refuse to see things as they really are, and to admit that they must coordinate their considerable resources to protect their investment in the community.

The old-time groups resent the new neighborhood development effort. This effort represents an end to the old order and poses a threat to people who have established themselves as being of some importance in these groups.

In accepting Negro leadership, for instance, the development effort has alienated many of the old-time leaders. As a neighborhood worker, I represent the "broadening influence," the new process, the integration of community resources. So I am resented.

The old clans are losing their grip; they are shaky, unsure. They know they no longer fit. They cannot accept the new effort but they cannot resist progress openly. So they resist and frustrate the effort secretly and subtly. They must be changed or shoved aside.

A newer kind of ethnic neighborhood is on the increase. This is the Negro gray area, the result of apartheid in our cities. Most of the residents of these areas are people with high standards, steady, modest incomes, and the determination to have good homes for their children to grow up in. These are people who have risen above the slums and are reaching hard for middle-class respectability. They cultivate lawns and flower beds. They modernize the kitchens in the old homes they buy, and put game rooms in the basements. These Negro gray areas are touched by physical deterioration, unemployment, and social problems of every kind — all the usual forces of decline made more intense by discrimination.

But they are peopled by rising, determined men and women. These areas can have a good future if their leaders organize and take hold of the resources of the metropolis. A Negro gray area in ferment will be looked at in Chapter 9.

The most attractive of the central city living places are the residential areas of faded elegance. Filled with old mansions and fine apartments, they exist on the fringes of some downtowns, usually near universities, medical centers, and other large institutions. The families are headed by professors, physicians, lawyers, administrators, and similar elite who work in the nearby institutions or downtown and send their children to parochial and other private schools. The convenience and attractiveness of these neighborhoods is so great — and the number of relatively high-income professional men in our society is increasing so fast — that there is a high demand for housing in such areas and a constant physical regeneration that is keeping this housing elegant and handsome. The residents of these areas have money and sophistication. They have influence and links through the whole metropolis. They know what services their areas need and how to get them.

Some of the most attractive examples of such neighborhoods are Beacon Hill in Boston, Society Hill in Philadelphia, Kenwood in Chicago, Homeland in Baltimore, Shadyside-Morewood in Pittsburgh, and the old private streets in St. Louis. There is a community cohesiveness in such areas, but it is often tinged with snobbishness. Residents are constantly fighting to maintain and improve these neighborhoods. They seek to prevent any conversion of large old homes to rooming houses, and to halt the encroachment of institutions and apartment buildings into their blocks of single-family homes. They regularly seek stepped-up policing to protect themselves from criminals who come out of surrounding low-income sections. Often they employ private police for night patrols. In some such areas, Chicago's Kenwood in particular, high-income Negroes have purchased homes and have been successfully integrated into the neighborhood. Kenwood is an area where residents have worked closely together and have developed a strong sense of community.

Expensive new town houses are going up and finding a ready market in these areas, as are apartments built on the periphery. For such neighborhoods to gain maximum benefits from physical development a master plan is needed. These areas can afford to provide their own plan if the city government does not. The neighborhoods of faded elegance, peopled by men and women of talent and wealth, have a great responsibility to furnish leadership for the whole city. As they furnish this wide leadership they grow in depth as local communities.

## Redevelopment Areas

Redevelopment areas are the newly rebuilt residential sections rising on land cleared by urban renewal in the central cities; places like Mack-Concord in Detroit, Prairie Shores and Lake Meadows in Chicago, and southwest Washington. They are striking to behold, with their highrise apartments and closely-packed town houses.

So far such new housing is expensive and mostly attracts single people and childless couples of high income. These are largely a mobile, sophisticated people who do not take quickly to forming closely knit communities. They are quite aloof from the low-income families who often live nearby in public housing. What neighborhood life may develop in the future remains to be seen. Like the shiny physical surroundings, a sense of community will probably have to be planned for.

There are some signs that community can begin to form. Independent political groups have been formed among residents of Chicago's Prairie Shores and Lake Meadows, and these groups generate some sparks of community. The majority of residents are young adults, many of them single, and there has been much socializing among them — a kind of easy communication — but transiency seems to prevent the roots of community from growing. Doorbell-ringing amateur politicians have found response in the Lake Meadows-Prairie Shores complex; a key club flopped. Though these areas have the ultimate in services, links to metropolis are through owners rather than through the tenant residents, and sense of community in the way of human relationships is small.

There will be many such redevelopment areas constructed in the future, and the kind of life lived in them will be important to the life of the whole central city. They may be little more than elevator dormitories for urbane, on-the-move people, or they could become much more. Needed is residential leadership willing to work at answering the question of what community means in a redevelopment area — and what it can be, and how to achieve it.

### The Postwar Tract Suburbs

Now we turn to the outlying residential areas of metropolis. These are the suburban areas of new housing and the old towns which once existed with considerable independence but now are caught up and shaped by the metropolis. The suburban areas may lie within the central city at its outer edges, or in separate little governmental units beyond. They are distinguished by their new housing, young white families, and style of life.

These are the great growth areas of America — now and for the foreseeable future. They have been ridiculed in song and book as split-level traps and habitats of organization men. They have been characterized as monotonous and homogeneous. With good construction, with a little neighborhood planning, such suburbs can offer a modest, decent home. When poorly built they become what Californians call "slurbs" — slovenly, slipshod, semi-cities. Some have no buildings except houses — all services are from outside the living area. Such suburbs are apt to be deadly and empty, with little chance for cross-communication among people, or the building of links to other sections and to the institutions of metropolis.

Whatever their character, tract suburbs are becoming the homes of most young families. The environment of these suburbs will shape a good part of our future population. Millions have made the choice, so that the task is not to destroy or abandon these areas but to develop them as the best possible cradles and local communities. They have newness, space, greenery, and vigorous residents. Their problems include lack of planning and tax money, and narrow racial attitudes. They seldom have the well-developed water, street, and sewer systems, school buildings, churches, and other facilities, built-up and largely paid for, that residents of the central city have.

Families of the small-house suburbs are struggling financially with mortgages and child-rearing. The taxes they are able to pay are severely limited. Many of these suburbs have little or no industrial or commercial property on which to lay a part of their tax burden. Housing designs lack variety and sites have not always been preserved for future public facilities.

Negroes were excluded from these postwar suburbs at the time they were first constructed and the houses sold off. And a quiet policy of exclusion has been informally maintained in most suburbs ever since. In a few, however, there have been Negro move-ins in quite small numbers during recent years, sometimes accompanied by white men's violence and mob scenes. Today under the surface of all such suburbs there is a haunting fear that Negroes soon will try to move in. As the education, income, social expectations, and militancy of Negroes increase, and fair housing laws become more numerous and better enforced, the number of move-ins is going to increase. Planning is needed to ensure the dispersion of these move-ins so that no suburb will be turned into a new ghetto.

Suburbs are growth areas. They can be what their developers, residents, and governmental officials make them. They can achieve through citizen action and planning the essential neighborhood qualities listed at the end of Chapter 2. Or they can be left to drift into "slurbia." Imaginative action — whether it be enlarging the tax base by allowing some industry in a corner of the suburb, or by joining with nearby municipalities for joint effort — is called for.

The story of the suburb is the story of the young American family on the go. Here is a typical story, told by Mrs. Claire Campbell, a New Jersey mother of six:

> Seven years ago, after living in Park Forest, the gigantic housing development south of Chicago, we were transfered to the New York area. Loaded with dreams of unconverted Manhattan Brownstones, converted barns in Connecticut, and large Victorian homes in Westchester, we went house hunting.
>
> Our first two dreams were quickly dispelled but we lingered over the third quite awhile. In Westchester we found several sixty- or seventy-year-old houses with one bath, four bedrooms, obsolete kitchen, ancient plumbing, and archaic wiring for twenty thousand and one-third down.
>
> After looking for several weeks, the real-estate people found out we had several children, were paying on a Chevy, and had only fifteen hundred dollars to our name. They suggested we work our respective parents over for a few more thousand and come back.

While searching for a house, we were staying with grandparents in a nice old Westchester place. They were well known and active in their community. Grandma had even baby-sat for several young couples in the neighborhood — but during the eight months we lived there only one couple (newcomers) even asked us over for a cup of coffee. We looked at each other one night and laughed. Why? We had been through the same thing in a Chicago apartment and finally against our wishes moved out to Park Forest — where we had enjoyed the year and a half more than any other time of our marriage.

We had found lots of struggling young couples there the same age and in the same boat we were. It was easy to get into any organization or activity. There was lots of back and forth visiting in homes.

Finally, however, we found our place, thirty-five miles from New York City. Exit nine on the New Jersey turnpike, Lawrence Brook Village, East Brunswick Township, New Jersey. Our house cost $17,990 in 1956. It has four bedrooms, one and a half baths, basement, one-car garage and is on a 100′ x 145′ lot.

The New York express bus stops a half block from our house and takes forty-five minutes to an hour (non-rush hour) to mid-Manhattan. Our state university is five minutes by car and the Newark airport (for my bi-weekly traveling husband) is thirty minutes down the turnpike. The good Jersey beaches are an hour away. The Pocono lakes and mountains are two and a half hours and Washington, D.C. about four and a half hours.

There has been room in the Catholic school for all our children so far. We have a new parish in East Brunswick and hopes of a regional Catholic high school. There is an active Boy Scout group, Little League, and other organizations.

Battles launched by the old settlers' angry Lawrence Brook Civic Association have given way to the Republicans vs. the Democrats. Through the churches and politics many of our neighbors have lost their tight-little-island existence. The present mayor of the township and several local officials are from our new development.

But there is still much petty competitiveness between the many different developments. Our section's people are still referred to as the "Smart-alec Madison Avenue Bunch."

Contrary to the latest paperback book and woman's magazine there is very little socializing in a given block or two except at Christmas time. The old close friendships, cliques, parties, and big intellectual discussions of the first years of moving in and planting lawns have given way to a polite friendly existence which, except for an occasional fight over child- or dog-damage is much like that of other older neighborhoods. And yet if you'd like to share a cup of coffee, get a ride to town, or have a couple in for cards there is a freedom and variety of choice that you don't have, or would be less likely to exercise, in an older, more conventional neighborhood.

The disadvantages of our development are (1) necessity to drive or ride to church, school, stores and library. (2) Monotony of architecture and lack of trees. (3) Little variety of income and age in immediate neighborhood. (4) Insufficient high school facilities.

We see here the young family's need for community expressing itself as a home is established. We see the failure of the suburb as a service district. We see the need for links to help overcome these things. We have here the cycle of the suburb. New families move in, visit with each other freely as they establish themselves, and then, feeling secure and at home, settle into a quiet routine pattern. One feels the presence of a vigor that could turn any suburb into a fine neighborhood community. Organization of suburban people seems to come easy. If honest, realistic planning and broadening of viewpoints can be part of such organization then it should become possible to make modern neighborhood communities of suburbs, and perhaps even smooth the way for racial integration.

Social scientists who have studied the suburbs, men like political scientist Robert Wood and sociologist Roland L. Warren, see families moving there in search of a return to small-town ways. Wood concludes that many families believe they can find in the independent municipality a more vigorous local community with active political participation. Warren sees families moving out of the city to escape the "great change" of urban life, that is, the growing complexity which has made the neighborhood less and less a self-contained unit. (It is ironic that so many suburbs turn out, as far as services are concerned, to be even less self-contained than central-city neighborhoods.)

There is in such motivation, of course, both strengths and weaknesses: strength in the urge to be part of a human community; weakness in the belief that such a community can and should cut itself off from the rest of metropolis. The suburbanite whose goal is to preserve small-town values and small-town ways rather than to build a modern urban neighborhood which is a well-functioning piece of the metropolitan whole, creates frustration for himself and additional divisiveness for the metropolis.

The tract suburbs provide homes for families of modest means. Some families are there to stay, and will go no farther up the economic ladder. Others, on the way up, will live in the tract suburbs only until they have the income to move on to the ultimate goal — the plush suburban village.

## The Plush Suburban Village

The handsome, idealized living areas of America are the gracious suburbs of large lawns, mature trees, and expensive homes. Some are all new, but the majority, certainly the most attractive, are blends of new and old — the Fox Chapels, Wilmettes, Grosse Pointes, and the rest. Their populations are small and their influence great.

While the tract suburbs are carefree and informal, at least on the surface, the villages are staid and governed by protocol. They are in some ways the suburban counterparts of the areas of faded elegance in the central city, and residents of the latter often move to the plush villages.

The people of such areas have high standards. Planning is usually well supported. All the needed services are supplied. Their links to metropolis are strong, as in the central-city areas of faded elegance. Suburban villages are important as style-setters for most families of the nation. They are the pace makers copied by other living areas. Their values are crucial in setting the tone of life in the whole metropolis.

Books have been published in recent years dealing with the psychological problems of the families in these areas and the social pressures of their way of life. Questions are raised about the degree of community developed in such areas. Particularly is this question raised in Maurice Stein's *Eclipse of Community,* which summarizes and comments on a number of neighborhood studies that deal with wealthy suburbs.

Stein presents a frightening picture of living areas where all material comforts are supplied, but where basic human relationships are strained, even chaotic. The play time of children is routinized and families find that the schedules of various members leave little time for intimate moments. Anxious mothers, no longer with the time and confidence to rear their children, turn to experts. Children are expected to display a good family image in their relations with their friends and other families, rather than establishing genuine, relaxed human relationships.

Housewives, taught to desire careers, are trapped in the home. Husbands, trapped in careers which drain their best energies, must look forward to a fate that has become as dreaded as death — that of retirement and free time. Looking ahead to their own prospective life cycles, the children soon learn to submerge the specter of a life that lacks rooted values and creative meanings by throwing themselves into the struggle for status. All of the vital roles wherein the human drama used to be played out — mother-son, male-female — now tend to be leveled. Their specific contents which had previously made them into channels for realizing a particular set of human possibilities have been bartered away for an ephemeral and empty sense of status. Not to perform these roles is to lose one's place but, sadly enough, performing them can never give one a place.

Stein reduces plush suburban life to an extreme, but his exaggeration helps us see the ultimate ruin that can come to a society that is broken apart, communityless, a society where ordinary human qualities have a low priority. There is a problem here that goes far beyond the scope of this book — a problem of the human being turning into a mere object of schedule and display. The solution would seem to lie in a reordering of man's life in accordance with his true nature. A neighborhood with a strong sense of community, where basic human values are highly respected, could help families achieve such a reordering. The challenge in the suburban villages would seem to be not so much land, buildings, public services, and links to the metropolis, as it is love, peace of mind, and human community.

## The Old Towns

Outside the boundaries of every large central city are

numbers of older towns and boroughs which in appearance and problems are much like the gray areas of the core. Industry and old store-buildings mix with old housing. There is crowding, obsolescence, ugliness, vacant stores, and all the rest.

There are also some strengths and weaknesses which do not exist in the gray neighborhoods of the core. Such towns are self-governing living areas. This means their governments can be close to the people; participation is often much easier for citizens. Many ordinary residents become public officials on a part-time basis. Many important decisions on taxes, public works, zoning, and the like are freely debated by citizens at meetings of the governing bodies.

There is on the other hand often a self-centered outlook. This may be partly the result of such conditions as a severely limited amount of property on which taxes can be raised to pay for public works and services. Gray areas of the central core have all the vast resources of a large city government to aid it. The old town has meager resources on which to draw. These towns often have the advantage of large amounts of open space, so that building of new housing and industry is possible. Some old towns which had large amounts of vacant land available at the close of World War II have in effect been turned into new suburbs by the postwar housing boom.

Most old towns face the same need for renewal as do the gray neighborhoods of the core. The merchants of an old town's Main Street are in trouble as are the merchants of the shopping street in the old central-city neighborhood. Churches in each have lost membership. Schools in each need modernization. Neither is laid out to handle the large numbers of automobiles now in use. The old town needs the same vigorous leadership by politicians and citizens, and the same large doses of physical and social renewal as do the central city gray areas.

* * *

These six types of neighborhoods are not the only residential places in the metropolis. There are the little rural settlements hidden in outer metropolis, the lively little Bohemian sections of the core, and others. These six, however, are the most numerous and contain the great mass of the population in any metropolis.

One matter of growing importance in a metropolitan society is accessibility between neighborhoods, and particularly between outlying areas and the central core. The core serves outlying neighborhoods by furnishing to their family heads the opportunity to earn a living, and to the whole family the cultural facilities to broaden mind and spirit. Accessibility means adequate expressways, sufficient off-street parking downtown, and fast, comfortable, convenient mass transit. Few metropolises have these things. The result is that many suburban neighborhoods, in the words of Leland Hazard, are becoming "cultural deserts." Many children are growing up with little knowledge of the wonders of human creation and diversity that are available in the core. The federal government is now beginning to put vast sums into modernizing public transit, and it is here that the best hope for improved accessibility lies.

The making of a local community out of any piece of metropolis is no easy task. Many men are attempting it. As they succeed, the urban place better serves its true purpose as an environment that promotes the dignity of the person. There is no single formula of renewal that can be applied to any and every piece. The strengths, weaknesses, and peculiarities of each must guide the making of a unique plan for that area. Different kinds of neighborhoods need different kinds of strategy to achieve the services, links, and sense of community and integration essential to a successful modern neighborhood.

In this chapter and the last one we have looked at the pieces of metropolis as they are. There has been much said about what is desirable. Now we turn in the next several chapters to what is being done. We move from problems, opportunities, and goals to methods, means, and solutions. Out of the armchair and into the struggle.

Let it be restated here that a well-ordered neighborhood is not the end-all and be-all for urban man. It will not serve all his needs. It will not provide him with all the means to develop his talents. He also requires a well-ordered family, metropolis, and work environment, among other types of communities. The neighborhood is only one of the communities in which he lives. It is one, however, which can be of great aid to him.

# Chapter 4

# HYDE PARK-KENWOOD: GRAY AREA IN TRANSFORMATION

Reversing the decline of an urban gray area is about as easy as halting a runaway bus with bare hands. Fortunately, there are courageous and imaginative citizens and public officials willing to use their bare hands and all the tools available. Efforts at revitalization are under way in many gray areas. Only a few of these efforts have been going on long enough to allow for a judgment of the results. One of the most advanced is the large-scale effort to revitalize the Hyde Park-Kenwood neighborhood of Chicago.

This complex undertaking has been scrutinized, analyzed, damned, and praised in books and articles since shortly after it began in 1949. I worked as a staff member for two of the neighborhood's key citizens' organizations during the crucial years, 1951 to 1959, and have kept close to the neighborhood's development since. I believe the unfolding story of Hyde Park-Kenwood is of great significance — for its mistakes as well as its achievements. I was involved in making some of the mistakes and in ignoring some of the needs, and therefore have no qualms about discussing failures along with accomplishments.

Actually, the effort has been so extensive and complex — over seventy thousand people, a major university, thirty thousand homes and apartments, plans for three hundred million dollars' worth of demolition and new construction have been involved — and the results so mixed, that anyone writing about it can probably find some evidence to support any position he wants to take. Reaction to the effort may be praise, condemnation, or puzzlement, but there is no doubt that it is one of the nation's most important tests of whether a slipping, aging urban living place can be transformed into a modern neighborhood.

Hyde Park-Kenwood is not a typical neighborhood. It is a place of extremes, contrasts, and intensity. Like a laboratory it provides maximum stresses and strains for testing the tools, the matter, the participants of a gray-area renewal effort.

Here are Chicago's Osteopathic Hospital and College, the National Opinion Research Center, some of Frank Lloyd Wright's magnificent early houses, the world famed Museum of Science and Industry, the renowned Sonia Shankman Orthogenic School, national headquarters of the American Bar Association and of the American Public Administration Service. Here comedians Elaine May and Mike Nichols got their start, Enrico Fermi performed the first controlled release of atomic energy, Louis Wirth carried out his pioneering social studies. It has long elected the city's only independent alderman. The neighborhood occupies two square miles of choice land along Lake Michigan on Chicago's South Side, fifteen minutes by rapid transit rail line or Outer Drive expressway from the city's downtown.

For the first half of this century Hyde Park-Kenwood was an attractive, stimulating living area, its residents enjoying the lakes' beaches and breezes, tree-lined streets, well-maintained apartments, spacious houses and elegantly serviced hotels. Retired schoolteachers and married graduate students on modest budgets lived around the corner from high-income professionals and some of the city's wealthiest families.

The area sparkled with a bit of arty, Bohemian flavor that originated with the Columbian Exposition of 1893, and had been kept alive by students, faculty, and followers of the dominant institution, the University of Chicago. Learning, research, creative work preoccupied many of its seventy thousand residents. For instance, play-reading clubs abounded, members meeting regularly in each other's homes. Its population has never been more than two percent of the city's total, but it has been a two percent that has done much to bring vitality and controversy to a city whose neighborhoods, up to 1949 at least, were chiefly noted for plodding placidity or aggressive racial exclusion.

Racial change was the overwhelming reality on Chicago's South Side, in 1949 as today. In that year ghetto-slums to the north and west began seriously to affect Hyde Park-Kenwood. Some genteel upper-income families sold their large Kenwood homes or allowed leases to expire on tastefully furnished apartments, and quietly moved to the fashionable North Shore suburbs, or to "safer" neighborhoods farther south. In even larger numbers moderate-income families slipped away from the three-story apartment buildings which dot the neighborhood.

There had long been a small, relatively stable Negro population living in some sections of Hyde Park-Kenwood. In 1949, Chicago's exploding South Side ghetto rolled up to the neighborhood on two sides and spilled over. Whites of all income levels became acutely aware of this movement and lived poised for possible evacuation.

Migrating Negroes triggered flight for many white families. But other negative forces helped to shape their decision. The climate of affluence following World War II led middle-class people to expect high standards in their living environment.

They expected quality schools, abundant parking

space, safe streets, ultra-modern kitchens, color-tile bath-
roms, bright shopping centers, and green foliage. Hyde
Park-Kenwood by 1949 had been falling away from these
standards for many years. Its narrow streets were
swamped with automobiles. Many of the apartment buildings were shabby and old-fashioned, inside and out.
Schools were overcrowded, with little or no playground
space. Aging shops were strung out in long ribbons on
a half dozen streets, with many store rooms empty, or
relegated to such secondary uses as warehousing, light
manufacturing, rowdy taverns. Streets were dirty, buildings soot-encrusted, lawns trampled, and trees disappearing.

In 1949, neighborhood leaders, of whom Hyde Park-
Kenwood has always had a large supply, became alarmed.
These were clergymen, professors, housewives, lawyers,
black and white. They saw the threat of Negro inunda-
tion, with speculators cutting up houses and large apartments into numerous, second-rate "kitchenettes," street
crimes multiplying, despair and flight of stable families,
a deadening of the intellectual atmosphere. They foresaw
eventual destruction of one of the most lively (i.e., most
human) local communities in Chicago.

Under the initiative of several neighborhood churches,
citizen leaders mounted an offensive, forming new organizations and reinvigorating some old ones, and began
a localized movement of urban development that used
block organization to ease white-Negro tensions, enforcement of housing laws to check cutting up and overcrowding, political action to gain new legal tools, and stronger
local elected officials to prevent manipulation of school
district boundaries to keep schools all-white, and finally
neighborhood-wide planning and urban renewal.

The neighborhood leaders who took the initiative in
1949 were upper- and middle-income residents, most of
them liberal intellectuals. Their goal was set forth in a

slogan adopted early in the effort: "an interracial community of high standards." The new citizens' organization they formed — the Hyde Park-Kenwood Community Conference — has kept its program aimed at this goal ever since. Although the University of Chicago eventually gained direct control over the urban renewal planning, the renewed community that is emerging today clearly reflects this original goal. The operating funds of the Conference came from residents, foundations, neighborhood businessmen, and small institutions, none of it from the University.

In the first years of the renewal effort, Conference leaders made repeated attempts to gain the active support of the University administration for their conservation and rebuilding attempts. While many faculty members were active as individuals, the administration long remained on the sidelines. Finally, in 1952, with a new chancellor, Lawrence Kimpton, at the helm, and neighborhood conditions (particularly crime) affecting the University's ability to attract quality students and faculty, the University stepped in on its own terms, formed its own neighborhood association, and put greatly increased muscle and power into the effort. The University's goal was to protect its own interests, a parochial but quite legitimate goal, and one of great importance to the city of Chicago and the whole nation. The University of Chicago is a major strength of the Chicago metropolis.

The joint effort of residents and University proceeded on what was then a bold new concept: to use planning and renewal for saving an existing community, rather than for tearing the neighborhood down and starting over. Also unique at the time was a neighborhood going to government to seek renewal, rather than having local government impose a program. The united neighborhood forces — residents, university, businessmen, churches and other institutions — won the support and cooperation of city government. By 1954 urban renewal was the major development tool being used in Hyde Park-Kenwood.

Citizens sought through use of this drastic tool to make the area so modern and attractive that it could retain its vitality, continue to hold and attract high-standard white and Negro residents, and thereby establish the city's first successful interracial community; the University hoped to gain land for expansion and an environment where it could continue to flourish as one of the world's great centers of learning and research.

This locally conceived urban renewal program moved in two stages. The first stage was clearance of a small, heavily deteriorated section in the heart of the neighborhood. This project served several purposes: it knocked down some of the most overcrowded eyesores; wiped out twenty-three taverns, thereby solving much of the area's liquor-control problem at one swipe; it provided a large piece of land for a new shopping center, apartments, and town houses; and, most important, it boosted morale by proving that drastic change was possible.

While the dramatic renewal program moved forward, citizen self-help efforts held the community together. Thousands participated. To mention a few:

Madeleine Hudson, Kenwood housewife, labored long hours operating from her home a housing information service which sought to keep the homes and apartments of her section in single-family occupancy and out of the hands of speculators and converters. She died of a lingering cancer, working to the end.

Louis R. Silverman, a tough, sophisticated volunteer politician helped give the neighborhood strong, liberally orientated elected officials. During campaigns he would often work himself — and friends — all through a night, his towering 6'4" frame inevitably topped by a large black hat.

Victor Towns, a dining-car waiter, who spent his at-home days building a block club organization that insisted residents care for their property, and fought off encroachments of the University on its land. When railroad depression ended his job, he became a real-estate broker and found new, imaginative ways to help build up the neighborhood.

Herman Cohn, clothing store merchant, who stayed in Hyde Park-Kenwood and expanded his business when others were fleeing. When many were afraid of Negro customers, he welcomed them. When urban renewal tore down his store, he rented a larger one in the new shopping center. When last heard from he was president of the Business and Professional Men's Association, and chairman of the Outer Drive Committee of the Conference.

Stage two of the renewal effort was the making and carrying out of a plan for the whole neighborhood. Stage two is well along, with limited clearance largely completed, and a promising beginning on modernization of the buildings to remain. The neighborhood plan on which stage two is based was developed by a planning unit set up by the University at the time it entered the renewal effort. City government lacked planners of its own, the University desired control, and citizen leaders went along with the University because they wanted the effort to move swiftly. There emerged the astounding situation of a major interested party doing the planning for a public project. Many citizens and government officials were to regret going along. Often they were to find themselves at a disadvantage when their interests or philosophy differed with the University's.

Fortunately, the University's chief planner was Jack Meltzer, not only an able professional, but a sensitive, patient man always ready to listen to neighborhood people, individually or collectively. He accepted their suggestions when they appeared sensible and practical, and did not conflict with the University's interests. A PTA and some allied block groups were able to persuade him to modify the proposed location of a school site. Residential parking lots were increased, a building here and there was added to or subtracted from the clearance list, and other changes were made at the request of citizens.

The planner established regular and frequent relations with citizens' organizations in Hyde Park-Kenwood, particularly with the planning committee of the Hyde Park-Kenwood Community Conference, which continually fed in suggestions, and critically reviewed each element of the plan as it was produced.

Because the University and most of the articulate residents who belonged to organizations were in full agreement on seeking a neighborhood of high standards, there was accord on most of the plan, including removal of much deteriorated housing, enlargement of school sites, relocation of a major street, and creation of numerous small playgrounds and parking lots.

Conflicts of interest on some matters did flair into fights between University and residents. The University wanted one large residential area turned into a research park. Residents wanted it kept for housing. Part of this area ended up as a center for emotionally disturbed children; most of it remained as housing. But the attempts of residents to cut down the ring of new institutional land around the campus were resisted. The needs of the University always came first. At one point the emboldened University sought to change the name of the neighborhood to "University City." Residents killed this in a hurry.

Because of lack of citizen initiative, the University was also able to gain control of the Community Conservation Council, a body of fifteen neighborhood people appointed by the mayor under state law to review and approve the plan. This made it even more difficult for residents to have their views prevail on disputed planning issues. The plan that finally emerged, however, came fairly close to giving them what they wanted. Residents, after pulling and hauling among themselves, asked that a limited amount of scattered public housing be included, feeling that provision should be made for some low-income families in the replanned neighborhood. The University and its planners said no, the project had enough obstacles to its success. The residents finally won a few units, but only a few.

An example of conflicting interests among residents themselves was the proposed enlargement of the Ray School site. To enlarge the site for additional classrooms and a sizable playground, required destruction of half a block of handsome, well-kept old homes. The planner proposed they be destroyed. The people involved belonged to a block group which met early and often to debate the issue. They themselves were divided. Most said: "This block epitomizes the very kind of high standard community we are trying to preserve through urban renewal." But a few dissented, saying, "If our homes are needed for the common good they should go." They went. Ironically, the land is still vacant.

Planning issues were explained and debated at almost three hundred neighborhood meetings, large and small, during a three-year planning period. These were meetings of block groups, church societies, neighborhood organizations, and mass public gatherings. Members of the Conference planning committee explained the emerging planning proposals at these meetings, and carried the criticisms and countersuggestions back to the University's planner. The planner was always sensitive to criticism and gave consideration to counterproposals, sometimes meeting directly with the advocates of such proposals.

In 1958 there finally emerged a Hyde Park-Kenwood renewal plan upon which most neighborhood interests were in general agreement. None were wholly pleased with it, but most were willing to accept it as the best plan possible. It took a sustained system of communications and evaluation operating between planners and people to create a neighborhood plan which met most of the needs of the neighborhood, and gained sufficient public support to be carried out. A public hearing on the plan before Chicago's City Council occupied five sessions and brought forth 150 witnesses. The whole metropolis received an education in neighborhood planning and urban renewal, as the hearing received widespread newspaper coverage.

Opponents of the plan, most of whom came from outside Hyde Park-Kenwood, found themselves facing a neighborhood desperately united, supporting the plan as the one way to keep their living area from becoming a ghetto slum. The opponents said the plan proposed to destroy too many sound buildings, would force the relocation of too many low- and moderate-income people, had vague standards for modernization of existing buildings, and overall was too expensive. Chief opponent was the Catholic Archdiocese of Chicago, which launched a sudden and unexpected attack on the plan after having been silent through the long years of the plan's creation. Supporters said the plan would preserve seventy-five per cent of the neighborhood's housing, help strengthen the city's tax base, point the way to renewal of all Chicago, and make possible the city's first stable interracial neighborhood.

The city council approved the plan unanimously, with a proviso that some public housing be added. The city's renewal agency, with strong cooperation and frequent needling from neighborhood citizens, institutions, and organizations has been working since 1959 to put the plan into effect. More than seven hundred buildings have been purchased by the agency and torn down. Three thousand families and two thousand single persons have had to move, most of them out of the neighborhood. Four hundred businesses have been dispossessed, and 145 of these have quit. Several dislocated merchants have banded together and constructed their own new shopping center at Fifty-third and Woodlawn.

Much of the cleared land has been sold by the agency and on it have sprung up contemporary town-houses, a child-care center, a fire house, convenient parking lots, and clever playgrounds designed by the City Park District with much assistance from the imaginative Parks Committee of the Community Conference. The neighborhood's two thousand or so privately owned single-family houses are in sparkling shape with orange, black, or red doors, carriage lamps, and modern kitchens. Property values are leaping upward. Some houses purchased for $18,000 or $20,000 in the fifties and modernized for $5000 or $10,000, are today selling for $40,000 or more.

Hyde Park-Kenwood today conveys a feeling of new openness and gloss. There is weed-filled cleared land waiting to be built upon, and plenty of shabby apartment buildings not yet remodeled, but the contrast with 1950 is sharp and dramatic. The twelve-year-old daughter of a friend summed it up when she said, "We're not a slum any more." This change has evolved out of agony, suffering both by those who fought to save their community from becoming a slum and by those forced to relocate (in some cases, the same people). One finds today some troubled consciences in Hyde Park-Kenwood, as well as new pride and hope.

Hyde Park-Kenwood now is more urbane than ever. Some of the arty flavor has been restored but it comes at a price, reflecting the more middle-class world that renewal has helped to create. Citizens have purchased over $100,000 in bonds for a nonprofit arts center to be established in the neighborhood under the leadership of the wife of the President of the University. The hope had been that low-rent shops and studios could be provided for struggling young artists of talent. But construction costs and lease requirements of mortage holders appear to be such that few but financially prosperous artists will be able to move in.

There is more off-beat, legitimate theater than ever. The *Hyde Park Herald,* community newspaper, is fatter, its circulation up, and its columns full of lively neighborhood events and controversies. A typical issue might include exposure of a dubious private real-estate deal, announcement of a public tour of Kenwood gardens, latest word on a battle to determine whether cleared land along Forty-seventh street should be rebuilt with inexpensive town houses or a mixture of inexpensive and expensive, an editorial attacking practices in a neighborhood political campaign, a debate on inadequacy of police protection, and the story of an eagle's attack on a Hyde Park-Kenwood dog.

The University is thriving, has purchased and modernized many apartment buildings and hotels for student housing, and has built a number of new buildings of its own. It still, however, seems to draw resentment and suspicion from many neighborhood people, especially Negroes. There remains the feeling the University wants to run the neighborhood on its own terms, that it only reluctantly accepts the biracial character of Hyde Park-Kenwood, and has not contributed sufficiently of its enormous resources to the revitalization effort.

One prominent Negro real-estate man puts it this way: "The University has missed a tremendous opportunity to put the skills of its faculty, students, and services to work for the social renewal of Hyde Park-Kenwood. It has never seemed concerned with the people and isn't now. It seems only interested in protecting itself.

Instead of driving people out by urban renewal, we should have been helping them to develop job skills, and to learn how to live in the city. We've pushed a lot of problem people into other neighborhoods." This man's criticism applies as much to the citizens' organizations as it does to the University.

Even more remarkable than the dramatic physical rebirth, is the relative racial stability of the neighborhood. The population is about evenly divided between white and Negro after more than fifteen years of change. Every other neighborhood on Chicago's South Side in which racial change has begun since the war has become completely segregated within three to five years. This continued biracial character is probably Hyde Park-Kenwood's most certain sign of success. It has an imperfect character, to be sure. There are all-Negro sections and all-white sections, apartment buildings occupied only by whites, as well as interracial blocks and interracial buildings. For Chicago, even this imperfect character is an extraordinary achievement.

The upgrading of the neighborhood's housing in condition and price undoubtedly has aided the building of an interracial character since Negroes of middle- and upper-income are limited, and integration is more easily achieved under high social and economic circumstances. The expensive new apartments and town-houses built on land cleared by urban renewal have been integrated with particular success. But the consciences of many long-time neighborhood leaders sting today because there are fewer and fewer modest apartments within financial reach of the retired schoolteacher or struggling newlyweds.

There are other problems that remain. The public schools still do not have the quality of education and racial balance to meet the neighborhood's goals. There are upwards of two hundred converted buildings whose owners are reluctant to modernize. Slowness of apartment building owners to modernize has brought charges of "unsatisfactory progress" against the project by the federal controller-general, who watches over urban renewal expenditures for Congress. As in most of Chicago, people are fearful of walking the streets of Hyde Park-Kenwood at night. There are some who complain about the ugliness of the new buildings. While there are two new shopping centers with large parking lots, residents in several sections complain there are not enough corner grocery stores left where a quick loaf of bread can be purchased at night or on Sunday.

The changes and improvements that have occurred, however, are so great that morale is up. A sense of well-being has settled over many citizens. At the same time, paradoxically, community organizations like the Conference find citizen participation down, and much of the old fire of civic leadership waning, as the sense of urgency declines. This weakening of civic fervor affects the sense of community. The generosity of volunteer effort is diminished. One public official, concerned with the weakening of community organizations, warns: "With city government firmly implanted like an institution within the neighborhood, many of the traditional citizen organization efforts have become eclipsed. This is unfortunate. At some point the network of governmental powers that function within the heady phrase, 'urban renewal,' must be withdrawn. How will the vacuum be filled? No organization is prepared to pick up the marbles." The question also arises as to whether neighborhood renewal is not a continuous process which once begun in a gray area, never ceases, so that there always remains some responsibility for local government.

Organizations that offer direct benefits to their members — the new Hyde Park Federal Savings and Loan Association; the Neighborhood Club, which offers recreation, day-care and adult education services; and the Hyde Park Co-Op which operates the neighborhood's largest supermarket — are flourishing, and tend to strengthen the community; participation in them, however, does not always represent the same militant spirit of sacrifice as is often found in community organizations. The Co-Op's expansion is a good example of how certain aspects of neighborhood life have grown with renewal. In 1949 the Co-Op's store had sales of $750,000. In 1965 they will be over $5 million. In 1949 the Co-Op was owned by 1200 families and their numbers were declining; today there are over 8,000 owner-members and the number is increasing rapidly.

Social planning and human renewal did not proceed concurrently with urban renewal in Hyde Park-Kenwood, as is the case in more recent neighborhood renewal undertakings (see Chapter 9 on Homewood-Brushton). Not as much was known about renewal when Hyde Park-Kenwood began, and the tools of social renewal like manpower retraining, juvenile delinquency grants, and the war on poverty were not then available.

In recent years Hyde Park-Kenwood has begun to do more about social renewal. The Neighborhood Club has opened a full-time study center where neighborhood children can find quiet and tutoring help. The Conference has a teen-age job program. More such programs are being planned, especially for the Negroes who occupy most of the unmodernized apartment buildings. Some of the youth participating in these programs come from the ghetto-slums surrounding Hyde Park-Kenwood. There are neighborhood leaders of broad vision who hope their affluent neighborhood can take more such responsibility for the disadvantaged areas nearby.

Hyde Park-Kenwood is the runaway bus brought under control. But it is not yet running as its passengers would like it. And it doesn't have a single driver in whom all have confidence. It has always had many drivers, and still does, which is probably one of its fundamental problems. The University has been a driver, as have been the alderman, the Conference, the City Department of Urban Renewal, and to some extent, the *Hyde Park Herald*. Each has its staff, its service office, its goals for the neighborhood, and outlets for communication. The unity of effort that comes from a single over-all organization and staff has been lacking and still is today.

In spite of all its shortcomings, Hyde Park-Kenwood has probably done as much on its own to stop decline and become a strong, modern, neighborhood community as any gray area in the United States. Its physical revitalization is amazing. Its services generally are greatly improved. Its links to the metropolis, especially city government, are firm and are being utilized.

Had those who opposed the Hyde Park-Kenwood plan in 1958 been successful in stopping it, the neighborhood would have probably become just another bleak, crowded, low-income section like dozens of others in Chicago. What these opponents did not seem to realize was the irreplaceability of Hyde Park-Kenwood. To scatter its people, its art galleries, its restaurants, its colleges, its university, its independent political groups, its research organizations, and the numerous related enterprises, services, and traditions would have been to cut out part of the heart and imagination of the central city.

Citizens and institutions in Hyde Park-Kenwood know what they have been fighting for: a unique community that took almost one hundred years to develop, and one that would take another hundred to build up somewhere else if it were scattered to the winds. To keep intact and rejuvenate their community was the great common goal that kept citizens and University together through difficult, sometimes torrid, controversies — a unity that dumbfounded opponents.

For those who might wish to read in more detail about this unusual neighborhood and its development effort, there are two books which tell the story in great detail, and from differing viewpoints. Julia Abrahamson was the founding executive director of the Hyde Park-Kenwood Community Conference. She spent seven dedicated years building the organization and the neighborhood. With great optimism she has written a history of those years in *A Neighborhood Finds Itself* (Harper, 1959). The second book takes a much more critical view. Done by two disinterested sociologists, Peter Rossi and Robert Dentler, it is entitled *The Politics of Urban Renewal* (Free Press, 1961). Mrs. Abrahamson treats the primary matter: neighborhood efforts for survival and renewal. Rossi and Dentler concentrate on an important, but secondary question: Who made the planning decisions and how were they arrived at?

The final word of appraisal on this fascinating neighborhood is yet to be written. There is no doubt, however, that already we can learn much about the making of a neighborhood community from the experiences of Hyde Park-Kenwood.

# Chapter 5

## RACIAL INTEGRATION: THE STORY OF SPRING HILL GARDENS

In walking the streets of an urban neighborhood — no matter what its shape, style, or income level — race tension comes quickly to the surface in even the most casual conversation with white householders. Whether it be a central-city neighborhood already mixed racially or an exclusive suburb ten miles from the home of any Negro, apprehension is present.

It can take a little while for a white man to discover the resentment among Negro householders. The tension is there also, however, deep-seated and burning, since it is an affront to any man's dignity to know there are others who believe he is not fit to dwell among them. And when this affront means that you live among squalor and your children go to third-rate schools, then the resentment is multiplied.

Racial mistrust is probably the most flagrant and persistent disturber of the peace in urban neighborhoods. This state of tension is born out of the tragic history of Negroes in America, a people with deeper American roots than nearly any group in our society. The Negro was brought to America in filth and chains and forced to live in a state of degradation. Although legally this bondage ended a hundred years ago, the white man has continued to identify the Negro with slave conditions ever since — conditions of dirt and ignorance, of violence and immorality.

87

Dennis Clark in his book on race and neighborhood, *The Ghetto Game,* calls this association "the white man's fantasy." The most terrible aspect of this fantasy has been its tendency to be self-fulfilling; that is, as white men have continued to think of the Negro as a slave in squalor, they have taken actions to keep him that way. Today the Negro is in revolt against this fantasy and all the customs and devices that support it. We are seeing in this nation a revolution of dignity, pushed forward by determined people, who will eventually destroy the fantasy.

One of the most difficult places to destroy it, perhaps the final stronghold where apartheid will make its stand, is the living area. We have seen the enormous effort necessary to establish even a quite imperfect interracial neighborhood in Hyde Park-Kenwood. A further revealing view of the fantasy under fire can be had from looking at the history of the Spring Hill Gardens development in Pittsburgh.

Spring Hill is one of Pittsburgh's many hillside neighborhoods, isolated from the rest of the city by deep valleys. It has narrow cobblestone streets, crowded with small spic-and-span houses, and is peopled largely by families of German and Austrian background whose roots in the locality go back three or four generations. It has three small churches, its own school, a thriving savings and loan association, and a bustling clubhouse of the Workmen's Beneficial Union. In 1949 a Negro family attempted to move in and was stoned out.

In 1957, ACTION-Housing Inc., Pittsburgh's civic organization concerned with increasing the supply of moderate-income housing and rejuvenating aging neighborhoods, initiated a plan for new apartments there. Four of ACTION-Housing's board members and its general counsel formed a nonprofit corporation to carry out the project, which was destined to shake up life in tidy, placid

Spring Hill. This nonprofit corporation planned and put under construction 209 apartments financed by a special federal program. The nonprofit corporation named its project Spring Hill Gardens after choosing a large tract of vacant land on the very top of Spring Hill.

Construction of Spring Hill Gardens proceeded through 1958, with first occupancy set for April 1, 1959. This construction brought mental turmoil to Spring Hill people. Drastic change was upon their neighborhood, and they did not like it. The feelings of neighborhood people, and steps taken by ACTION-Housing in reaction to those feelings, are reflected in these notes of mine made after meetings between Spring Hill citizen-leaders and ACTION-Housing officials in 1959, as the date neared for the first families to move in:

> This first meeting was in the aging Spring Hill School, where we arrived after a torturous drive up steep, old-world streets. When we met the bus coming toward us we had to pull over to the curb and let it pass.
>
> Fifteen worried citizens, each the leader in a neighborhood church, veterans group, or social club were gathered around a table in the school library when we came in. They were quite friendly in shaking hands.
>
> A young woman from the City's Commission on Human Relations chaired the meeting. First came reports from two of her research assistants who had been interviewing and studying the neighborhood. It was a cold beginning. They poured forth a blunt sociological profile of the Spring Hill neighborhood, including its "lower than average educational level."
>
> Then we got down to immediate business with Bernard Loshbough, of ACTION-Housing, answering any and all questions. Citizens' fears began to come out.
>
> They asked if the 209 apartments were to be low-rent public housing, rather than nonprofit moderate rental housing. They asked if every apartment would

be occupied by Negroes, if the schools wouldn't become overcrowded, if already woefully short facilities of the neighborhood streets and playgrounds wouldn't be severely overtaxed.

They revealed themselves as homeowners who feared renters, as families who had been in the area for generations and feared strangers, and as whites who feared Negroes.

Asking their questions, they were surprisingly moderate, polite, unemotional people. The ACTION-Housing director carefully explained the civic nature of the development and its purpose as a demonstration of how new moderate rental housing might be achieved for people — all people. He explained how such new government-aided housing must be open to all; then pointed out that the nonprofit corporation had a goal of no more than two or three Negro families in each building of eleven apartments, with a plan to carefully screen every applicant, white and Negro.

Fears of the citizens were calmed somewhat, but not completely. Plans were made to meet again in two weeks.

Second meeting tonight. Smaller group of citizens this time, but two or three strong-minded men who seem to be real leaders, and seemingly willing to seek a working relationship with ACTION-Housing and the Commission on Human Relations.

We first discussed the common needs of the neighborhood, particularly for recreation facilities and more sewers.

A committee of residents was appointed to look into the question of a permanent organization and to come back to the next meeting with recommendations.

Then came more questions about Spring Hill Gardens. These concerned screening procedures and rent levels, fears being expressed that tenants cannot be found to pay the rents of $75 to $95, with the result that rents will have to be lowered, leaving insufficient income to maintain the building in decent shape.

Strange thing about these rents. We know they are very low for new housing — $10 to $15 lower than comparable new housing elsewhere in Pittsburgh — but Spring Hill people are accustomed to rents of $40 to $50 for the smaller apartments that exist on second and third floors of older houses in the neighborhood. There seems to be a resentment, perhaps subconscious, toward families who can move in and pay $95 per month for larger, better quarters.

The race issue was touched upon in some of the questions, but did not burst out. It is obvious, however, that it is always there, under the surface.

One of the men, a telephone lineman who owns a newer house in the neighborhood and represents a Protestant church, told about being on a walk around the neighborhood last Sunday and meeting a Negro couple who had come to look at the new apartments. He said he was impressed at how well dressed the Negroes were; he spoke to them and they told him they wanted to move from their all-Negro area because "a lot of lower-class people are coming in."

After he told this story, the president of the PTA at Spring Hill School stood up and told how one-third of the presidents at city-wide PTA meetings are colored and what smart, cooperative women they are.

Both of these testimonials impressed those present, and cleared the air somewhat. The air was cleared even more after the meeting, when coffee and plates of pastry were produced and we all stayed around to become acquainted.

At future sessions between citizens and representatives of ACTION-Housing and the Commission on Human Relations, neighborhood opposition to the apartments gradually turned to reluctant acceptance as citizens became convinced the development would be occupied by carefully selected tenants, the amount of racial integration would be moderate, and existing school facilities would be adequate to handle the increased load.

Just before the apartments were occupied, an open house was held for people of the neighborhood. Hundreds came to see and admire the modest but modern apartments. Coffee and doughnuts were served, with neighborhood women acting as volunteer hostesses. The party was marred only by a premature exhaustion of doughnuts.

With staff leadership from the commission a permanent community organization grew out of the continued meetings with citizen leaders, and the monthly agenda soon switched to recreation facilities, street repairs, and a polio clinic for the whole neighborhood. This organization increased the sense of community in Spring Hill. And in time it even came to have a Negro member, one of two tenants of Spring Hill Gardens who came to represent the tenants' association. The Spring Hill school was integrated without incident for the first time, a good example of integrated school flowing from integrated neighborhood. A vast replication of this pattern is needed in our time when the neighborhood school is under attack because urban ghettos have resulted in many Negro children being segregated into overcrowded schools.

A new supermarket was built in the neighborhood, partly as a result of the new apartments, and this provided all of Spring Hill with a much needed service. The residents' committee established links with a settlement house and with the city planning department and began to work seriously for many other needed services, including better access roads to other parts of the city.

The great change wrought by the apartments opened up a hidden neighborhood to communication with the whole metropolis. And not only did Spring Hill benefit but some of the skilled leadership in Spring Hill began to serve the whole city by representing the neighborhood on city-wide committees.

As the apartments opened on May 1, 1959, the goal of the sponsors was two or three Negro families in each of the nineteen buildings. This goal was established after consultation with many specialists, including the staff of the Pittsburgh Urban League. There is no doubt that had the apartments been opened without planning for racial balance they would have soon been occupied only by Negroes, and probably would have led to white flight from the neighborhood, with Spring Hill becoming another ghetto.

Renting of the apartments went slowly from the beginning. The racial integration was probably the greatest barrier, but the isolated location, and high rents (relative to older apartments of the same size) also were factors. Aside from some name-calling by teen-agers roaring by in cars, the apartments opened without racial incident. They have been kept rented at about 90 per cent of capacity through the years. Door-to-door surveys of tenants have been made every six months, and no dissatisfaction has ever been found with integrated living. The goal of two or three Negro families per building has been maintained.

A month after the apartments opened, Pittsburgh's new fair-housing law, prohibiting discrimination in the sale and rental of housing, went into effect. The following year, 1960, two qualified Negro applicants for apartments filed complaints with the Commission on Human Relations because they were asked to postpone their move-in date until there were sufficient white applicants to maintain the established balance. The Commission on Human Relations asked that they be offered apartments immediately. An apartment became available for each complainant, however, prior to their cases reaching the public-hearing stage.

The president of the Spring Hill Gardens nonprofit corporation stated at that time, in a speech to the National Urban League: "We have been able to comply with these orders without upsetting or typing the development. But we know our community, and we know Pittsburgh. If this law is to be used to force us to accept more and more Negro tenants until the percentage reaches forty or more, then Spring Hill Gardens will be on the way to becoming a segregated development; a panicking neighborhood will result; and the cause of race relations, housing, and urban renewal will all be considerably harmed." Since that time there has been space for all qualified applicants within the sought balance, and no test of this prediction has arisen. It may arise in the future. The sponsors intend to obey the law. It is probably unfortunate that fair-housing laws are not flexible enough to provide for situations of this kind, where men of good will are attempting to prevent segregation by a policy of a balanced community.

There is a paradox here and perhaps even what would seem to be hypocrisy. Planned racial balance itself is considered an offense against their dignity by many Negroes at the same time that it gives them the opportunity to live in dignified housing free of segregation. Planned integration is a tool whose use would seem logical to achieve good neighborhoods, but it must be used with great care, sensitivity, and integrity. In Spring Hill there would very likely have been violent opposition to the opening of the development had residents not been assured of the goal of limited integration. And it is very likely that few white tenants would have ever moved in without this assurance.

Spring Hill Gardens has demonstrated — as have a number of other interracial developments — that integrated living under high standards can be successful. The white man's fantasy gives way under the impact of planning, real facts, and firm action.

# Chapter 6

# NEIGHBORHOOD POLITICS: THE ABNER MIKVA CAMPAIGN

Political leadership is a key ingredient in neighborhood development. Unless there are mayors, city councilmen, county commissioners, township supervisors, precinct committeemen, state legislators, congressmen, governors, and even a President who understand the needs of the living area, many barriers will stand in the way of development. A major element of leadership will be missing.

Without competent political leadership adequate services will not be forthcoming for a neighborhood. The effectiveness of the links between a neighborhood and the various levels of government depends in good part on the interest and responsiveness of elected public officials. The wisdom and charity with which a living area faces race relations often depends on the courage of political leaders. School budgets are usually determined in the political arena. So is the quality of fire protection, the making of street repairs, the amount of money going into job retraining and urban renewal efforts, and many other matters related to neighborhood life.

A sense of community can be created by the unity and purpose given a neighborhood by strong, unselfish political leadership. Much of Hyde Park-Kenwood's spirit has come from its independent aldermen, who have included Paul Douglas, now a U.S. Senator, Robert Mer-

95

riam, who became a top staff member for President Eisenhower, and the incumbent, Leon M. Despres, who almost single-handedly has kept dissent alive in Chicago's city council.

Political power depends on votes, and votes are cast on a geographic basis. People vote where they live. Therefore, political parties have had to seek to organize votes through neighborhood workers: ward chairmen, district committeemen, and precinct workers. These carry the political wars into the neighborhood, which becomes the crucial battleground for basic campaign functions: acquainting voters with local candidates, identifying "plus" voters (voters on your side) and getting plus voters to the polls on election day.

The political structure runs unbroken from national committees in Washington to the neighborhood block where the precinct worker labors. The situation is healthy when both parties have active workers in every block. One-party cities — the typical situation being inner-city areas where only Democrats are active and suburbs where Republicans hold complete domination — retard democracy and community growth.

The quality and role of political leadership has varied greatly in American cities. In a city like New Haven the regular political process has produced strong and competent leadership which makes itself felt down to the neighborhood level. In a vast urban complex like Chicago effective political leadership at the neighborhood level has been more difficult to come by. Citizens have often had to take matters into their own hands, as in the election of Hyde Park-Kenwood's aldermen, and some state legislators.

A few years ago there was a significant legislative campaign involving Hyde Park-Kenwood and two nearby neighborhoods, South Shore and Woodlawn. This campaign put the relationship of political leadership and neighborhood into sharp focus. I was personally involved in the campaign and feel that it illustrates, among other things, what neighborhood people can do for themselves within the American political system. It also showed how a deeper sense of community can be built by a political campaign participated in by large numbers of neighborhood people. The story is one of aroused responsibilty and grubby door-to-door work.

This campaign originated after a reapportionment of the Illinois legislative districts, the first in fifty years. Several dedicated political amateurs, members of the Independent Voters of Illinois, from the three South Side neighborhoods, sensed an opportunity. Completely new legislative districts were being established.

Many of these citizen politicians had long been unhappy about the poor quality and lack of vigor of their state representatives. In Illinois, as in most states, such representatives hold great power over cities — controlling their welfare and education purse strings, their taxing powers, and many other fundamental matters. The group was concerned particularly about the new Twenty-third District containing the neighborhoods of Hyde Park-Kenwood, South Shore, and part of Woodlawn. They decided to try to insure that at least one of the district's new representatives would be a man of outstanding energy and ideas.

Over a period of several weeks they examined records at the Election Commission's office, evaluating voting habits in the new legislative district, precinct by precinct. Each Illinois district is entitled to three representatives, and they found this one likely to elect two Democrats and one Republican. They decided to seek the election of a topnotch man to one of the Democratic seats.

They found four potential candidates capable of giving the district strong leadership. One was a college professor who had once run for Vice-president of the United

States on the Socialist ticket; one was the former director
of the National Council of State Finance Directors; one
was a bright young newspaper publisher; and the other
was Mr. Abner Mikva, a young labor lawyer who had
assisted legislators in the writing of bills, knew state
issues well, and had been active in neighborhood organizations in Hyde Park-Kenwood. After finishing law school
he had served as law clerk to a justice of the United
States Supreme Court.

To give the Democratic Party the benefit of all doubts
these four possible candidates were introduced to the
ward committeemen from the three neighborhoods. These
committeemen are the ward political bosses. Their word
is final on the slating of legislative candidates — and
ordinarily slating means automatic nomination. The
amateurs told the committeemen that if they would pick
one of the four there need be no primary fight. At the
same meeting the committeemen introduced the amateurs to their own candidates. Committeeman James
Ryan of South Shore announced, "These two men of ours
are thoroughly qualified by their long service to the party
as faithful precinct captains." And that was it. The amateur candidates were out, as far as the regular organization was concerned.

The neighborhood people fought among themselves
for a couple of weeks, and united around the labor lawyer.
He could match every asset of the other three candidates
and had labor manpower and finances to support him.
Petitions were circulated, and the name of Abner J.
Mikva was filed for the spring primary against the two
regular Democratic candidates, a Mr. Banks and a Mr.
Kinnally. Many "sophisticated" persons told the neighborhood amateurs they were foolish, since "you can't
beat the Chicago regular Democratic organization," and
especially not in a primary when the turnout is small

and most of those who do vote are the loyal followers of Party precinct captains.

The amateurs and their candidate were only spurred on to prove their point by such advice. They formulated a hard-hitting strategy — maximum face-to-face exposure of the candidate with voters, and systematic door-to-door work in every block of every precinct by volunteer workers. Their problem was an immense one. Voters in large central-city neighborhoods are not attracted much to primary campaigns for local offices, especially when the candidate is an unknown. Attracting attention, turning the attention into interest, and the interest into votes represented a formidable, if not impossible, task.

Leaders of the Independent Voters of Illinois recruited every member and every friend in the three neighborhoods to become canvassers to organize the vote. And they brought in enthusiastic carpetbaggers to help. I was one of these, and participated in a typical precinct effort.

The whole campaign became a great ninety-day project in neighborhood education and neighborhood organization. Mikva set up headquarters for the Hyde Park-Kenwood area on Fifty-fifth Street. It also became his central headquarters for the district. A large candidate's calendar was maintained by some of the volunteer office girls in the central headquarters; it usually showed that Mr. Mikva had three coffee parties per evening, and morning handshakes at the bus stops and Illinois Central train stations, plus luncheon appearances before neighborhood Kiwanis and businessmen groups, and afternoon dates with women's organizations. The Mikva headquarters, through the help of some Republicans who didn't mind at all seeing a good squabble in the Democratic primary, had obtained lists of the Democratic voters in all three neighborhoods.

I was assigned to assist a young Loyola University

professor work his own home precinct in South Shore. The first thing we did was to get up a coffee party in his home, to which we invited all the Democratic voters in the precinct.

Twenty-one voters came to the party. Mikva was impressive with his razor-sharp talk about judicial reform and neighborhood conservation. After he left for another meeting, the twenty-one sat around with cake and coffee, and it was clear his presentation had given us a collective foot in the precinct's door. This was the prelude to the weary weeks of ringing doorbells and talking Mikva, in order to identify a limited number of plus voters.

The opposition in this campaign — the regular organization — was experienced and well heeled. Its experience, however, told it that amateurs get nowhere and primaries are easily controlled. So its workers moved sluggishly, expecting to roll to an easy victory.

Mikva continued to grind away at the parlor circuit, getting every friend and friend's friend in the three neighborhoods to set up a party. A few people were disappointed to learn that even if elected state representative he wouldn't be able to do much about immigration laws or social security benefits; but his enthusiasm and knowledge and the whole fantastic notion of beating the regular organization began to take hold. Mikva's persistent pushing and the door-to-door backup began to get the message across. A real crash project in neighborhood education unfolded successfully. Many citizens began to understand that the quality of neighborhood life was somehow involved in the election of Mikva.

All of the independents working in our South Shore neighborhood gathered in the store-front headquarters on Seventy-first Street five nights before election, heard some pep talks from a prosperous junkman (who loved independent politics and was the independent ward chairman), from Mikva himself, and from Alderman Leon Despres.

We were told there were 166 precincts in the whole district and if they could average 100 votes a precinct for Mikva we had a chance to win. Everybody had their poll lists along and most could not count enough pluses to be sure. We had to face the unpleasant reality that twenty precincts in one neighborhood were not being canvassed by any Mikva workers. We were told that all of the precincts in the other two neighborhoods were covered. The junkman announced that the Sunday before election he would throw a bagels and lox breakfast at his home, "Bring along some friends," he said, "and we'll get those other twenty worked." About thirty showed up, and went out and worked the untouched precincts.

The last few days, precinct workers sent reminder postcards to all plus voters and called on some of the doubtfuls; on the last day they went around and handed all the pluses a sample ballot showing how to vote for Mikva on the voting machine.

In Illinois the polls open at 6 A.M.; so workers were on hand about 5:30 A.M. to meet the first voters. It was a biting cold morning. As each voter came to the polling place workers gave him a cheery hello and handed out a sample ballot. The regular organization captains came along to assure our workers they were wasting their time.

The professor and I polished off three cups of coffee each and gave out thirty-nine sample ballots before early morning voting slowed down. We went into the polling place and checked on which of our plus voters had not yet come in. The organization captain confidently predicted, "The vote's going to be under a hundred, and they'll mostly be my regulars." Then we went out to hunt down any of our pluses who might be home and who had not yet voted. We were well aware that our fellow amateurs were doing this all over the three neighborhoods.

By 2:30 P.M. there were only seventy voters in — and not enough of them our pluses. We started an all-out drive. School children started coming home. Babies started waking up. The sun came out. Housewives got the urge to do some shopping. Doorbell ringing began to get results. Around 4:10 there were so many strollers and baby buggies around polling places that voters had a hard time walking in and out. The total jumped to over 100 in our precinct. When the election flag came down and the door was locked at six, the total was 131.

The final vote in our precinct was:

| | |
|---|---|
| Mikva | 68 |
| Nathan Kinnally | 40 |
| Sanford Banks | 23 |

About 7:00 P.M. the South Shore independents gathered in the Seventy-first Street headquarters. With two Democrats to be nominated, Mikva was running first or second in nearly every precinct. Word from the Mikva headquarters in each of the other neighborhoods was even better. One report received by phone from Hyde Park-Kenwood told of a retired schoolteacher who brought in 436 votes for Mikva. The crowd at headquarters grew larger and noisier as excited amateurs talked to each other about their day's experience. The climax of the evening came with the announcement of the total vote for the district:

| | |
|---|---|
| Mikva | 20,378 |
| Kinnally | 17,808 |
| Banks | 11,639 |

In the actual election, in November, Mikva again rolled in first, in spite of some regular Democrats who were unhappy about having a rebel on their slate. After entering the legislature, Mikva took the lead in introducing bills to outlaw discrimination in housing, to prohibit overcrowding of rooming houses, and to revise the state's oppressive wage-garnishment statute. Through the years he has had a profound effect in improving the quality of a traditionally mediocre legislature.

Chicago citizens were given new hope by this campaign, and the city's neighborhoods still reap the benefits. Citizens of the three neighborhoods where the campaign took place became much more concerned with social and physical renewal of their areas. Many of the active amateurs of this campaign became leaders in over-all neighborhood renewal efforts. The sense of community was greatly enhanced in the three neighborhoods.

# Chapter 7

# SUBURBAN GROWTH: THE CASE OF NORTHWOOD ACRES

The only living areas presently showing large and sustained growth in America are the suburbs. There are a few inner-city redevelopment areas here and there that are gaining people, but except perhaps for some of the new apartment sections in Manhattan, the quantity of people that are going to be attracted to redevelopment areas is not large. Seldom do the new populations in redevelopment housing match the teeming numbers that occupied the same land areas prior to redevelopment.

The suburbs contain over fifty million persons now and will likely triple in size by 1990, while farms, rural villages, towns, and central-city cores will continue to decrease in population. If for no other reason than sheer numbers, then, the suburbs are of immense importance to the future of the nation. But there are other reasons, one being that these areas offer Americans some of the small-town qualities for which they yearn.

The chief element of a suburb, often lost sight of, is its "subness"; it exists near a large central city, and is dependent on the central city for jobs, higher education, entertainment, and many other things that make life possible and zestful. A perceptive editor of a suburban newspaper in the East has written, "a suburb without a city ceases to be a suburb and becomes a line of homes along a highway a long way from somewhere." It can also be said that a city without suburbs ceases to grow.

The average suburb is a residential place where younger adults with economic stability are attempting to find a pleasant way of life. They have chosen to find it here because of the American dream that equates newness, space, grass, trees, absence of factories, with the good life.

The growth of a suburb from a clump of new houses on barren land to a warm neighborhood community requires many things from many people. The physical qualities of a suburb depend primarily on the wisdom, vision, and skill of the local government controlling the land on which the suburb is built. Wise and firm control can achieve planning and a high standard of house construction. It can make sure streets are adequate and attractively laid out, that water supplies and sewer systems are sufficient, that schools and shopping and playgrounds and all the other facilities are provided, and that land is kept vacant for future needs like parks, schools, churches.

Physical excellence also depends on the home builders and developers, on their foresight in planning, their integrity in building well, their restraint in setting fair prices. A sense of communty depends on the generosity and leadership of the families who move in, and upon the depth of the institutions they develop.

Links to governments and other outside resources are in some ways more complicated for a suburb than for the living areas of the central core. Central-core neighborhoods can draw help from the single large city of which they are a part. The suburb, small and somewhat isolated, must draw upon a township, a county, or a school district — resources that are more scattered and remote. The success of a suburb and its people in establishing these links is a key determinant of its social and physical development and well-being.

As for integration, openness, variety of people — the lack of these is the great, largely ignored threat to future well-being of the suburb. Today suburbanites live in a fool's paradise, with the racial time bomb ticking slowly but surely.

A middle-income suburb that has probably tried as hard as any to become a strong neighborhood community is Northwood Acres in Hampton Township, Allegheny County, Pennsylvania. Northwood Acres lies in a lovely rolling pocket of land north of Pittsburgh. All of its 110 homes have been constructed since 1956 and sit comfortably on half-acre lots. There is space for another forty or fifty homes, but the choice land has been built upon and little additional building goes on now.

The 110 houses range in value from $17,000 to $35,-000. A couple of new homes have been unsold and vacant for some time, and in this era of geographic and economic mobility there are always twenty to twenty-five for sale. A few homes are being rented. Values are down about $2,000 from original purchase price and this is a matter of discouragement for many. Five or six of the properties have begun to look tacky, with the lawns neglected and outside painting behind schedule. Neighborhood leaders feel this is partly the result of the burden of caring for large lots: some people finally just give up. The leaders have been squeamish about saying anything to their neglectful neighbors. Their response to the problem is a silence they may in time regret.

Northwood Acres homes have large mortgages. Their would-be owners are successful salesmen, middle-grade executives, engineers, scientists, with a sprinkling of other occupations includng a major league ball-player and a couple of men temporarily unemployed. Incomes range from $7,000 to $25,000, with the majority between $9,000 and $14,000. All residents are white — a fact whose significance the neighborhood has not yet faced.

This small pocket of community is near St. Ursula's Catholic School and more than half its families are Catholic. The usual pattern is for all children to attend the same public kindergarten and the same public high school with the Catholic children off on their own for grades one to eight. This is a possible cause of enrichment at the same time as it is a potential generator of separateness. One element of unity in Northwood Acres is the political party affiliation, which is 80 percent Republican. The development has no walking-distance shopping facilities.

In the suburb's years of founding and building up, from 1956 to 1960, there was frequent, easy, and informal communication and much socializing among households. As the neighborhood has shaken down, its families, many of whom came from other states, have shaped their friendships into a limited number of stable relationships and there has been less and less visiting between families. This pattern of early and easy acquaintanceship, with much running between homes, followed by a gradual settling down, is the usual experience in new suburbs.

Northwood Acres families have done more than most suburbs to maintain the early spirit, however, by forming a neighborhood association which has kept alive some neighborhood-wide socializing, communication, and joint effort on common problems. The Northwood Acres Association has, in effect, institutionalized community effort, making this something more than the effort of a number of individual families acting on their own. The Association sustains and feeds joint effort and builds a sense of community. Leaders of the Association and their families can move away but the leadership is replaced and the Association goes on.

The Association facilitates communication by publishing a small neighborhood newspaper six or eight times a year. It facilitates social life by sponsoring a number of events including a spring dinner-dance (the wives wear formals and keep alive their youthful spirit; this is part of the suburban mores — suburbs reflect the passion of Americans to maintain youth, newness, and vigor); there is a summer picnic, an ice skating party, a square dance, and a fund-raising game party. All of these events are well attended.

Each time a new family moves into Northwood Acres a housewife member of the Association appears to welcome the newcomers with a freshly baked cake. A special series of recreation affairs are run the year round for teen-agers. Specialized group activities have begun through the Association, including a garden club, bridge group, and a bowling club. The Association even maintains a community punch bowl which members may rent for their personal parties at a nominal rate.

The Association has been strictly a private voluntary organization with no paid staff member to organize or service it. About 90 percent of the families pay $5.00 a year to belong to the Association. One of the biggest projects undertaken has been the leasing and improving of a three-acre field for baseball and picnics. Hundreds of volunteer man-hours plus one rented bulldozer went into building the ball diamond and picnic facilities. A tree-planting project achieved almost 100 percent participation, with cooperative buying of a scientifically selected variety of tree at the rate of two per house. These were planted at the curb and in the years ahead will result in greatly increased beauty for the neighborhood.

Ambitions at one point soared toward a $25,000 swimming pool but neither interest nor resources were ever quite strong enough to transform this dream into reality.

It was found that some families already belonged to pool clubs in nearby townships. There simply were not enough interested families to support a pool.

Northwood Acres is a small community within a township of 10,000 people. It has swung political weight far beyond its size in the township because its residents have been organized. Only the township's volunteer firemen and Little League fathers rival Northwood Acres Association in organizational effectiveness. One of the most important tests of a local community comes when it faces a crisis — an important decision and fight. The Northwood Acres Association has faced two.

First came the great tank-farm battle, to which Northwood Acres citizens responded with zest and imagination. This crisis came when a large oil company purchased options on land in Pine Creek Valley just below Northwood Acres. The main line of the Baltimore and Ohio Railroad runs through the valley. The oil company planned to build a "farm" of gasoline storage tanks which would be filled from a nearby pipeline. Trucks would carry gasoline from the storage tanks to service stations in the whole district.

The land in question was zoned for industrial use because of the railroad and consequently the tank farm was legally permissible. Any trucks coming in and out of the "farm," however, would have to cross residential property, and for this a zoning change was needed. This gave the Northwood Acres Association an issue on which they could fight and an opportunity to stop what residents quickly decided was a dangerous and improper use, in spite of the additional tax revenues it would have brought into the township treasury.

The alertness of Northwood Acres people is illustrated by the way they learned about the tank-farm proposal, long before it became a public matter. One of the residents worked for a company that did business with a

trucking company scheduled to carry some of the gasoline. He heard about the contemplated tank farm by
chance, immediately sensed a possible threat to the
neighborhood, and aroused the people. This early notice
gave the Association time to prepare and wage a massive campaign of opposition. There was some fumbling
around as the campaign began but cool, experienced
hands came to the fore.

Petitions were circulated and more than 40 percent
of the township's families signed up to oppose the tank
farm. Few would have refused, but there was not time
to reach all. A research team dug out examples of major
fires that had occurred on tank farms in various parts
of the nation. Letters were obtained from appraisers and
banks on the ill effects a tank farm would have on the
mortgageability and salability of property.

At a public hearing before the township supervisors,
the Baltimore and Ohio Railroad testified to the dangers
of having loaded gasoline trucks crossing its tracks. The
pastor of the Catholic church spoke on the danger of his
school children. A township resident who operated tank
trucks in Tennessee testified on overloading practices and
the irresponsibility of drivers. Several residents objected
to the expected noise.

While the supervisors thought the matter over during
the days after the hearing, residents wrote to nearby gas
stations, threatening a boycott if the stations received
their supplies of gasoline from the new tank farm. Two
advertising men who lived in the neighborhood began
to prepare an ad against the project in the daily newspapers. Before the supervisors came to a decision, the
oil company withdrew its plan for the tank farm.

The second big issue was sewer rates. The builder
who developed Northwood Acres had constructed his own
sewage-disposal plant. Under state law, however, the per-
mit to build had to be issued to the township govern-

ment. This was done with an unwritten agreement that
the builder would put up the plant at his own expense
and eventually turn it over to the township cost-free.

After some wrangling with the builder the township
government took over the system. Up to then the residents had been enjoying the system without charge. The
township decided a fee would have to be charged if needed
repairs were to be made on the system, and if it were
to be operated properly. The township supervisors set
up a proposed schedule of fees and invited the articulate
citizens of Northwood Acres to discuss the question of
rates at a public meeting.

An engineer member of the Association made an
analysis of the proposed schedule and came up with figures showing the rates were double what they should
be. These were presented to the supervisors who took
the matter under advisement. At a second meeting the
residents offered to take over the system and run it themselves. The supervisors turned down this offer, but did
agree to cut the proposed rates 30 to 40 percent. The
residents agreed to accept higher rates at a later date
if a real need for more revenue could be shown by experience.

Each of these crises illustrates the effectiveness of a
neighborhood that is vigilant, that has knowledge and
energetic members. Regardless of the merits of the position they took, they did so for strong reasons backed by
competent research. The Northwood Acres Association
now sends an observer to all meetings of the township
supervisors, planning commission, and school board. The
Association is able to know about problems as they
arise. The Association has attempted to work with the
township school board on plans that would benefit the
whole township school system, just as in the tank-farm
battle the Association people led a fight on a matter

that affected many parts of the township outside North-wood Acres.

The total program of the Association, social and political, helps weld the people of Northwood Acres into a community. To date the Association has not entered into issues which involve county-wide questions — an involvement through which the skills and sophistication of Northwood Acres citizens could be put to work for the whole metropolis. Their interests have not yet been directly affected so as to motivate them on larger issues. Whether they respond when faced with an opportunity to assist on an important metropolitan issue remains to be seen. This would be a further test of the maturity of this suburban neighborhood organization.

The direction such associations take, whether they remain narrowly confined to immediate neighborhood issues, or raise their sights to metropolitan problems like race relations, unemployment, rapid transit, county-city relations and the like is going to determine in large part the future quality of metropolitan life.

# Chapter 8

# NEW APPROACHES TO CREATING STRONG NEIGHBORHOODS

The four previous chapters describe neighborhood efforts of determination and accomplishment, but efforts that are incomplete and partial. In none were the planning and action of officials and citizens of sufficient scope and force to gain the services and physical improvement, the links to metropolis, the diversity of population, and sense of community needed to make a strong modern neighborhood.

In Hyde Park-Kenwood sense of community was retarded by the people having too little control over the planning for their own neighborhood. Relocation pushed out many lower income people, insufficient low-income housing was provided, with a consequent decline in diversity.

Looking at Spring Hill Gardens we saw the partial achievement of racial diversity in an old urban neighborhood, but it was confined to one set of apartment buildings. Other neighborhood improvement efforts were limited. The bringing of some racial integration and the resultant formation of a citizens' organization to work at neighborhood development were but a beginning.

The Mikva campaign was a piece — but only a piece — of neighborhood development. Political action is important. But there are many other kinds of action that must be taken.

Northwood Acres was seen as a place where alert citizens were organized to preserve their handsome suburb and its middle-class way of life. They were, however, cut off from the rest of the metropolis. There was very little diversity of people, and no visible effort or desire to achieve diversity.

There is clearly need for a more comprehensive approach to making sound neighborhood communities out of troubled living areas.

Several new, serious attempts are being made by tough-minded, imaginative urban strategists to find such an approach. Four attempts, in particular, are significant and worthy of close study. These are large-scale, sophisticated development efforts. With powerful support from a variety of resources including foundations, churches, government, universities, industrial corporations, and citizens' councils, they are now being tested in the neighborhoods of several metropolises. Similarities and differences appear in these four new approaches, all of which seek human development and the creation of vital, modern neighborhoods. In all approaches the key pieces are citizens, resources, and professional staff. The importance of each piece and the manner of its movement on the urban chessboard vary widely from approach to approach.

The four approaches are:

1. The neighborhood conservation approach of New York City.

2. The social invention approach of new city-wide urban organizations supported by the Ford Foundation, including Action for Boston Community Development, Community Progress, Inc., of New Haven, United Planning Organization in Washington, D.C., the Interagency Project in Oakland, California, and the development programs in several North Carolina cities sponsored by The North Carolina Fund.

3. The self-determination approach of the Industrial Areas Foundation, with its principal test area in Chicago.

4. The neighborhood urban extension approach of ACTION-Housing, Inc., in Pittsburgh.

In the "neighborhood conservation" and "social invention" approaches the focus is on urban resources. These approaches seek to improve schools, state employment systems, legal aid, health departments and the like, and then, imaginatively and aggressively, to take these modernized services to neighborhood people. Their power base is money and government control. The neighborhood conservation approach comes directly out of city hall, the social invention approach out of a private, nonprofit civic organization closely allied to city hall.

The "self-determination" and "neighborhood urban extension" approaches put emphasis on citizens becoming alert, organized, and able themselves to locate and draw on the resources needed to build their neighborhoods. Both approaches draw money from elements of the urban establishment, as well as from neighborhood people. The self-determination approach draws on church dominations, labor unions, and government contracts. Neighborhood urban extension draws from philanthropic foundations, corporations, and government contracts. The main power base of both, however, is people organized in large numbers. A big difference is that the former follows a fight-city-hall philosophy, while the latter seeks a cooperative relationship.

New York City's neighborhood conservation approach was launched in 1959 in seven small living areas containing a total of one hundred thousand people. They were Chelsea, Bloomingdale, East Harlem, Carnegie Hill, Morningside, Hamilton-Grange, and Hudson. This is the only one of the four approaches operated directly by city government. Harry C. Harris, director of this New York City effort, has described its purpose: ". . . an experimental attempt to halt and reverse housing deterioration and meet and ameliorate social problems affecting essentially sound though troubled neighborhoods. The project was designed for areas which neither needed nor wanted formal urban renewal treatment, but required housing and social improvements to redress adverse trends and promote sound family life in what could become stable and vital communities."

As is typical in old New York neighborhoods, most of the people in the seven test areas were tenants in large apartment buildings. Essentially middle-income communities, each had a fairly new and significant proportion of low-income residents, many of whom were recent immigrants from the South or Puerto Rico.

When the program began, responsible property owners were selling out, mortgages for property improvement were difficult to obtain, housing laws were not being systematically enforced, overcrowding and deterioration of buildings were on the upswing. High traffic in vice and narcotics and increase in crime were causing panic among long-time residents. There was some racial violence. Services in the fields of health, education, recreation, and social welfare generally were inadequate. Newcomers, particularly, were not being helped. Neighborhood organizations and institutions were immobilized in the face of rapid changes, through desiring to do something. There was little communication among them and they lacked strength.

City government moved in to help these neighborhoods by stepping up public and private services and making these readily available from a neighborhood city hall; by having a settlement house, church, hospital, or university in each neighborhood sponsor the local program as a partner with the city; and by obtaining, through the sponsor, widespread citizen participation. The sponsors who were found raised funds from foundations, local businessmen, and neighborhood residents to help finance the program for the first two years. Setting up the local city halls, the sponsors hired professional staffs to operate them.

The director of the neighborhood staff became an unofficial neighborhood "mayor" whose job was to put to work and coordinate all the services of the city and private agencies. He had no legal power, but had to depend mainly on leadership and persuasive skills. A central staff from the city gave supervision to the neighborhood programs and fed in the housing inspectors, city planners, and other service specialists. After two years the city began to supply most of the financing, although the sponsors continued to supplement public funds, and take a strong partnership role. The city's aim from the beginning was to have neighborhood sponsors eventually take over complete management of the local effort, with city services continuing to be channelled into the neighborhood city hall.

Immediate impact was gained in each neighborhood through door-to-door surveys by city housing inspectors. Where large families were found living in one or two rooms, they were relocated, with an attempt made to solve their employment, health, and other problems during relocation. The first seven neighborhoods were used as action laboratories in which to devise, test, and then apply new housing, social action, public administration, and community organization techniques. Economic and racial integration was strengthened by modernizing some deteriorating buildings for use as public housing. This made it possible for low-income families to live under decent standards in nonproject buildings. Improved sanitation services, including daily garbage pickup and street flushings, were provided in all neighborhoods. Among some of the experimental services were a neighborhood narcotics rehabilitation center, and a diagnostic and referral service for elderly residents.

Staff and citizen volunteers aggressively went door to door, hunting out problems and seeking to organize tenants to help solve their own problems. Harris gives the objective for these tenant groups, and some evaluation of their progress:

> Nurtured by staff, the organizations were asked to help resolve problems affecting their buildings, their block, and finally neighborhood. Over a time, the campaign often resulted in motivating residents to raise their expectations; demand better service from property owners and public authorities; improve their own sanitation and housekeeping practices; take advantage of community facilities; and better understand and become more involved in various aspects of neighborhood life.

> Slow in developing, the projects were inhibited by personnel shortages, population mobility, lags in code enforcement, and the failure of staff and volunteers to bridge cultural and economic barriers.

While major planning, direction, and decision-making has come from city hall, the sponsoring agencies, citizen leaders, and volunteers have played a large role in identifying neighborhood needs and in helping carry out some services. Steering committees of citizens, organized by the sponsoring agencies, have given guidance to staff on many policy and procedural matters and actually become involved in the execution of some of the projects. Given a wide latitude in authority and responsibility, the citizen groups have in some cases exercised powers which are generally the province of public officials. Harris predicts, "as their knowledge grows and the neighborhoods improve, the steering committees will be strengthened and become the vehicles for rank and file participation in the future direction of each neighborhood conservation program."

Marked progress in physical and social development was made in Chelsea, Bloomingdale, and Morningside, with lesser progress in Hudson and Hamilton-Grange. The programs in Carnegie Hill and East Harlem have been unable to halt decline.

In addition to slowness in developing citizen participation, other difficulties were encountered in the seven neighborhoods. Relocation cut strong cultural and emotional ties for some families and brought social problems to the surface which could not always be remedied. Low-cost financing for modernization of buildings was not forthcoming. New construction of middle-income housing was not achieved. Success was incomplete in the sanitation program. Crime was cut, but gambling, prostitution, and, surprisingly, bootlegging, continued. Relations between the races improved, but housing segregation continued rigid. Techniques tried were inadequate for helping families in deep poverty.

In spite of these weaknesses, the neighborhoods were much improved over-all, particularly in condition of housing. Chelsea, Bloomingdale, and Morningside were saved from becoming slums and are now stronger communities than at any time in their recent history. They are now on their own. The city continues to put up half the money but has passed most operating responsibility to neighborhood agencies and residents. Each continues to receive counsel from a mobile professional staff, and has available to it city services which have been improved as a result of the experience in the seven neighborhoods. In time, Hudson and Hamilton-Grange are expected to develop sufficiently to be on their own. Due to intensive deterioration of housing and continually recurring social disorder, the futures of Carnegie Hill and East Harlem are in doubt.

KILROE SEMINARY LIBRARY
HONESDALE, PA.

This neighborhood conservation approach appears to have in it some promise for helping create strong neighborhood communities out of gray areas which have not yet passed the fail-safe point of deterioration and decay, and it demonstrates the need and wisdom of localizing municipal services. Its principal strength comes from the direct commitment of city government. Citizens play a limited role. They do not help plan the program, but become involved only after it is well along. Based on the broad experience gained in the seven pilot neighborhoods, New York City has changed methods, added services, and expanded the full program to two more living areas. A more limited program using the neighborhood city hall has been carried to thirteen other areas.

With the war on poverty program now providing greatly increased funds and personnel, this government-guided approach has considerable thrust. From the standpoint of testing a new approach, the New York City effort might be more significant if it were kept a city hall directed effort — with citizen partners — rather than attempting to shift the administrative responsibility to neighborhood institutions.

The second approach, which also puts emphasis on services furnished to people, is the social invention approach; it has been given large-scale support by the Ford Foundation and local foundations in each city where the approach is being tested.

The Ford Foundation has directly or indirectly put money into all four approaches described in this chapter, but its largest urban affairs grants have gone for this social invention approach.

Paul Ylvisaker, Director of Public Affairs for the Foundation, who has inspired and encouraged this approach, gives expression to its philosophy:

With an eye to the obvious, mayors, governors and presidents have concentrated their urban programs on physical renewal of the city's urban plant, usually beginning with the central business district.

Our hunch is that this is not necessarily the place to start, and is certainly not the place to stop. Crudely done, slum clearance and downtown redevelopment can actually harm rather than help the city's main business of producing first-class citizens. What the bulldozer in insensitive hands can mean to the residents of demolished neighborhoods is already painfully evident in the growing record of school transiency and residential displacement.

We have placed the Foundation's first bet not on the central business district of the city but on its school system, and more on school outlook and methods than on buildings; on the city and metropolitan area's employment system, on their administration of justice, and on a growing list of similarly critical "production processes" which are currently bottlenecks in the process of citizen-building.

Some of the innovations and improvements which suggest themselves are matters not so much of gadgetry but of spirit. The simple fact that improvements would even be attempted in institutions and neighborhoods long accustomed only to being neglected has peeled a couple of layers of hopelessness off the morale of gray area residents.

This second approach is carried out by new kinds of metropolitan organizations — "half-way houses" between the public and private sectors — on whose governing boards sit both government officials and representatives of private interests including business, industry, welfare, religion, labor, and education. Six such nonprofit organizations have been set up in Boston, New Haven, Philadelphia, Oakland, the District of Columbia, and North Carolina.

They have been granted a total of over $15 million

by the Ford Foundation, and some of them are administering many millions more from foundations in their
own cities, from war on poverty funds, and other federal
sources. These funds are used to reorganize and modernize old-line resources, particularly the public schools,
state employment services, health departments, recreation agencies, and welfare boards, so these resources
more realistically meet today's needs.

The courage and foresight of the Ford Foundation in
pouring millions of dollars into these projects has been
of great significance to urban development in the United
States. It has jolted public indifference to urban problems, and greatly accelerated the formulation and passage of the Economic Opportunity Act of 1964.

Local and state governments have taken the initiative
in beginning these new organizations, which are closely
allied with city halls and state capitols.    In working
to modernize resources, they have the leverage of
political power as well as Foundation millions. When one
of these new organizations loses its ties to city hall, as
has happened in Philadelphia, it becomes relatively weak
and ineffective.

These new organizations often operate by setting up
demonstration projects to meet needs in new ways, by
involving old-line resources in carrying out the demonstrations, and then by leaving the successful new ways
of operating to be adopted by the resources as standard
methods. New Haven's Community Progress, Inc., for
instance, has helped revolutionize the relation of the public school to the neighborhood around it by helping transform the neighborhood school into a community center
from which are operated programs in job training, senior
citizen recreation, home improvements, and the like. It
has made a grant to the New Haven School Board for
the appointment of special assistant-principals whose sole
duties are making the schools available to the whole

neighborhood through home economics classes for neighborhood housewives, recreational programs, opening of the school's medical and dental-examination facilities to all, development of the school building as a place for neighborhood forums and meetings, and other community programs.

Under this approach experts move into a neighborhood and begin to furnish imaginative new services to help people develop and neighborhoods improve. Some local people may be hired as staff assistants to help spread word of the new services to their neighbors. And citizen committees may be formed to help carry out the services.

The mayor of New Haven has described his city's effort as "a comprehensive program which goes to the root of the city's social problems [and gives] the people of our city the chance for much greater personal achievement." Oakland's city manager describes the purposes of his city's program: ". . . modern problems . . . are not structured as agencies are structured. Agency operations must, therefore, be reshaped to fit the shape of problems."

The new organizations pioneering this approach seek to end the tendency of urban places to treat needs of the sixties with methods of the twenties. Ylvisaker describes this approach:

> . . . their governing philosophy is to be stimulators of action rather than monopolists of action, to work through and alongside existing agencies whenever possible rather than to replace them. If these projects have no effect on the status quo, they will be an exercise in the useless and/or the unnecessary; it can't therefore be glibly said they offer no challenge to anyone. But the challenge, we hope, will be in the best tradition of American community leadership — which is to allow a mirror to be held up to reality, and to appraise what is being done in the light of an objective assessment of what needs to be done.

More than the other three methods described in this chapter, this approach takes a metropolitan view of problems, but it too finds the neighborhood the effective action area for most of its programs. In Boston, for instance, the major programs have been to organize citizens for participation in urban renewal planning, and to furnish employment and educational services for youth. The efforts at involving citizens in planning have been carried out at the neighborhood level in Charlestown, Roxbury, South End, Dorchester, South Boston, and Parker Hill-Fenway. For the youth opportunities project, action areas have been Charlestown, South End, and Roxbury.

Ylvisaker outlines some possible tasks for the new organizations:

> . . . social inventions can be immediately procedural, physical, and mechanical: e.g., building schools to double as neighborhood and social-service centers; starting the education of gray area children at an earlier age; concentrating on improvement of speech, reading, and other communication skills among Negro and other newcoming children; adapting techniques borrowed from agricultural extension work to the needs and circumstances of an urban clientele, in such areas as health, family budgeting and home management, legal aid, credit use, house repair and rehabilitation, and a variety of others; combining work and study programs for school drop-outs; relating and even subordinating physical to social planning; pooling local philanthropic funds for common programs — and I might add, wrenching philanthropy away from many of the easier, more traditional, and sanctimonious undertakings to which it has become fondly attached, to work at some of the really tough problems the modern urban community presents; recruiting industry and gearing vocational education to projections of technology and local manpower supply; early identification of urban newcomers; use of lay persons in school, recreation, welfare, and other programs; correcting abysmally bad practices in arrest, bail, defense, and other links

in the chain of administering justice; finding constructive alternatives to present systems of high-density
public housing and permanent-dependency welfare pay-
ments; and widening residential and occupational
choice as a way of releasing individuals from the chains
of ethnic, racial, and other attachments not freely
chosen.

Neighborhood citizens are encouraged and assisted
to organize as part of the social invention approach, and
their suggestions are listened to, but they seldom play
a central decision-making role. Their role seems to be
more one of communication and support. They do not
make the decisions on what services are needed or how
they are to be operated. They do become involved in
using the services, in getting other citizens to use them,
and in suggesting improvements. This approach seeks to
make first-class citizens through education more than
through decision-making.

Impressive results are being achieved by these new
organizations, particularly in stepping up the education
of deprived children and in job-training and finding for
youth. In some areas their service programs are broadening into over-all neighborhood development and are
closely tied into urban renewal and the war on poverty.
This is happening particularly in New Haven and Boston. As the vigor, imagination, and financial strength
of this approach are applied to over-all development we
will probably see many gray areas become strong neighborhoods. The cities where this approach has operated
well have been able to get a head start in carrying out
war on poverty programs.

The third approach is the self-determination approach
of the Industrial Areas Foundation (IAF) in Chicago.
IAF's approach is marked by conflict, militant action, a
stance of demanding from rather than working cooperatively with the resources of metropolis, and con-

siderable citizen involvement. IAF is a private, non-profit organization with headquarters in Chicago, which has received financing from the Presbyterian and Roman Catholic Churches, from private foundations, labor unions, and individuals.

Its staff organizers enter a neighborhood at the invitation of local groups, usually neighborhood churches. The organizers use the frustration and injustice of job discrimination, rent gouging, overcrowded schools, and similar issues to rally neighborhood people. Concentrating on the most deprived citizens, IAF workers create a broad-based neighborhood organization with local leadership. The organization attacks any outside force which exerts control over its neighborhood, and seeks to generate power to the point where it can control planning for the entire neighborhood. It demands and often gets what it wants from government.

This approach was brought into being in the late 1930's by Saul D. Alinsky, IAF's director, who helped labor unions and ethnic groups in Chicago's then depressed stockyards area to form the now famous Back of The Yards Neighborhood Council. Through the Council people achieved a neat and prosperous neighborhood with strong sense of community, firm links to city hall, and a rigid policy of racial exclusion. Today, Alinsky himself is critical of these two latter policies. He believes in racial integration under quota arrangements, and in neighborhood organizations being independent of city hall.

Alinsky and IAF are now facing their severest test in the Woodlawn neighborhood of Chicago. Woodlawn is a Negro ghetto neighborhood of solid, but overcrowded apartment buildings, heavy unemployment, high crime rate, schools that are unable to keep up with the needs of children, economic exploitation, and despair — but the citizen effort there initiated and assisted by IAF has dramatically identified, awakened, and brought to action these once discouraged citizens. They have been formed and educated by dealing seriously and militantly with their own problems.

When a Chicago bank refused to reveal the name of the owner of a Woodlawn slum building it held in trust, one hundred citizen members of The Woodlawn Organization marched into the bank, camped on the floor, and announced they would not leave until they had the name. They got it. When the Chicago Board of Education refused to transfer Negro students from overcrowded Woodlawn schools, The Woodlawn Organization formed truth squads to count empty classrooms in white areas, and then picketed the Board.

Appearing before a Congressional committee in 1965, The Woodlawn Organization made complaints against Chicago's war on poverty effort which shook the anti-poverty program from coast to coast.

Initiative and skills to form The Woodlawn Organization and shape its program have come from staff organizers of the IAF. Working with disdain toward other approaches to neighborhood development, IAF rejects many of the concepts and methods of city planning and urban renewal and insists that neighborhood people work out their own destiny by hiring their own planners. The Woodlawn Organization has attacked city government, credit merchants, slum landlords, and the expansion plans of its neighbor, the University of Chicago. The basic IAF philosophy is spelled out by Saul Alinsky, as follows:

> In the development of an organization for democratic participation . . . resentments and dormant hostilities must be brought up to visible surface where they can become transformed into problems. . . .

> . . . A people do not break through their previous fatalism of submerged resentment and frustration into

open problems which can be faced and dealt with,
until they have a mechanism or a formula for effectively coping with these problems. Since their only
resource lies in their numbers, organization becomes
the instrument for implementation of change and
resolution of these problems.

The Woodlawn effort has focused the attention of
city newspapers and city government upon a once forgotten living area. There is yet little concrete, visible
improvement to be seen in Woodlawn. There are, however, determined, organized, citizen leaders, formulating
plans and laying the groundwork for revolutionary
physical and social changes. The Woodlawn Organization
recently worked out a compromise plan with the University of Chicago and the city whereby the urban renewal tool will be used to clear a deteriorated area in
North Woodlawn, with one section of the cleared land
to be used for University expansion, and the remainder
for new middle-income housing for Woodlawn people.
Woodlawn citizens have control over planning to an extent never achieved by Hyde Park-Kenwood people.

Alinsky has appraised his Woodlawn effort thus:

> . . . an orderly revolution began in Woodlawn and The
> Woodlawn Organization came into existence as the
> representative group of the Woodlawn community. Its
> membership includes 83 organizations, involving with
> minor exceptions all of the churches in the community
> (and the very few church exceptions possessed little
> if any local membership), business men's associations,
> the block clubs, the fraternal groups, and literally every
> interest organization of any membership in the neigh-
> borhood. They have repeatedly and publicly demon-
> strated their representative character.

> A voter registration parade involving more than 45
> busses carrying more than 2000 persons was formed,
> and moved with that discipline and allegiance charac-
> teristic of an organization whose roots are deep in the
> lives of people. This was a dramatic public demonstra-

tion not only of a substantial popular support, but of the broad representative character of The Woodlawn Organization.

What kinds of words are used by the leadership? They use the word "negotiate" instead of "conference," or "sharing," and understand the meaning of the word negotiate. Negotiate means meeting with others as equals, since the other party will not negotiate unless it recognizes that you have the power to compel negotiations.

Mutual recognition of power is the necessary prelude to negotiation. In a meeting of negotiations the people enter with dignity of recognition as equals; they are not pleading inferiors, to be satisfied with less than their legitimate rights. They use the words self-determination, in the truest of American traditions and of Western civilization. They know the difference between citizen participation and robot ritual of agreement even if it is masked with so-called discussions.

The Woodlawn Organization has followed a policy of building internal strength by publishing its own newspaper (which has been at odds with the existing Woodlawn weekly), by operating an employment service available to members of its constituent groups, and by running its own private housing-code enforcement system, using the threat of picketing to force landlords into compliance with the code. The organization not only pickets landlords' homes but also their churches or temples while they are inside attending services.

If a group of neighborhood people come to The Woodlawn Organization for help with a problem, they are usually told to organize and affiliate first. The Woodlawn Organization seeks to be self-sufficient and independent. With Alinsky's strong urging, it is raising money to become financially free of IAF. Built as it is on a state of tension between neighborhood people and city government and other urban resources, the IAF approach raises questions as to how a sustained and responsible relationship is to be built between neighborhood and metropolis.

IAF seems to be aiming at some stable collective bargaining relationship similar to that which exists between labor unions and large corporations. The occasional use of militant, nonviolent action would seem to be quite necessary for an effective neighborhood organization. But a philosophy of sustained hostility would seem to endanger sense of community. For instance, a continual "fight city hall" stance could lead people to distrust local government and endanger a city's ability to raise taxes for needed services. Martin Luther King has made a success of nonviolent protest because he has been able to get his followers to take a stance of sustained love toward those against whom they are protesting.

Alinsky believes that a democratic society will always have many different sets of interests and that it is out of the tensions coming from conflicting points of view that we have the basic seedbed for creativity. He feels that to have a society in which you do not have a state of permanent tension is to have "a monolithic, totalitarian uniformity." Dealing forthrightly with controversial issues, building neighborhood power and using it militantly, and generating conflicting viewpoints would seem to be essential in beginning a development effort when the negative forces of deprivation, injustice, and discrimination are so intense and complex; but one wonders whether permanent tension between neighborhood community and metropolitan community, with one neighborhood demanding consideration above others, would not in the long run only worsen and intensify the negative forces.

A newspaper editor friendly to IAF has observed that unity of purpose and effort within the Woodlawn neighborhood has been possible because enemies — landlords, government officials, credit merchants, university administrators — were outsiders. Neighborhood people could unite against them. But in Chicago's middle-income Southwest Community, an IAF-initiated organization has not had the same striking, dramatic impact because it has lacked deprived people whose dormant hostilities could be aroused. Also, race baiters and the owners of substandard buildings live in the area. The enemies are within, making unity difficult. The final verdict on the IAF approach awaits the outcome of the efforts now under way in Woodlawn and other living areas of Chicago.

The fourth technique in this survey is Pittsburgh's neighborhood urban extension approach, built upon deep citizen involvement, and the modernization and utilization of metropolitan resources. Neighborhood urban extension has been created by ACTION-Housing, Inc., a metropolitan-wide citizens' organization, set up in 1957 to help carry out a broad program of housing development and urban renewal for the whole Pittsburgh and Allegheny County area. Its full name is Allegheny Council to Improve Our Neighborhoods-Housing, Inc. The author has been a staff member since 1959.

ACTION-Housing's program is a comprehensive one: (1) working with private builders and lenders to increase the supply of well-designed housing for families with incomes too high for public housing and too low for the regular private market ($4,000 to $8,000); (2) modernization of aging housing and neighborhoods; and (3) establishing a research base for future housing and neighborhood development programs.

ACTION-Housing's financial support now comes from consulting and research contracts, corporations, local and national foundations, and the Community Chest, with neighborhood people raising some of the funds for programs in their own areas. In 1957 funds came exclusively from the Community Chest, reflecting a wide community commitment to the organization.

The principal tool used by ACTION-Housing to aid private builders is its Pittsburgh Development Fund, a revolving loan fund which provides seed money for the construction of private sales- and rental-housing for moderate-income families, as well as the stimulation of large-scale home modernization. The Fund was launched in September, 1959, and given impetus toward its goal of $2 million by grants totaling $350,000 from the three Mellon Foundations. Subscriptions to the Fund have reached nearly $2 million in grants and interest-bearing loans from thirty-one local companies, corporations, banks, department stores, utility companies, and foundations. The desirability of loans to the Fund, rather than outright grants, has been emphasized. Two major housing developments have been put under construction through the Fund. The Fund is available for large-scale new construction and home modernization in urban extension neighborhoods. The Fund is a good example of the new kind of urban tool our metropolises need.

Through its Development Fund, ACTION-Housing already has helped establish a new neighborhood, East Hills Park, which has had a residents' association planned into it — a cooperative which has responsibility for maintenance of the grounds and outside of the now two hundred — eventually twelve hundred — homes. East Hills residents, who are racially mixed, work to solve various problems through the association, and in doing so are building a sense of community.

After several years of experimentation carried out with neighborhood groups, ACTION-Housing came up with the neighborhood urban extension approach to the revitalization of declining neighborhoods, an approach financed in part by a Ford Foundation grant, as well as by funds from Pittsburgh foundations, corporations, and neighborhood people. ACTION-Housing enters a neighborhood after being invited to do so by local citizens. A staff man, the neighborhood extension worker, helps citizens begin to understand complex problems, assists them to make plans, and helps them to get the vast resources of the metropolis extended into their neighborhood.

Bernard E. Loshbough, the executive director of ACTION-Housing, spells out the philosophy of neighborhood urban extension:

> More than bricks and mortar are involved in restoring and developing aging neighborhoods to their full potential. The strengthening and preserving of human values have fully equal importance.

> A cardinal principle is that when people share in planning, decision-making and carrying out their own program of renewal and development, they become imbued with a sense of responsibility and thereby gain a genuine sense of community.

The neighborhood extension worker assists residents, merchants, clergymen, industrialists, and representatives of neighborhood interests to form a neighborhood council which becomes the major instrument for local planning and action. A written memorandum is executed between ACTION-Housing and the neighborhood council. In the written memorandum an equal partnership in decision-making is provided for, and the full rights and responsibilities of each partner are spelled out, including joint responsibility for fund raising. Before an extension worker is assigned to a neighborhood he is first interviewed by citizen leaders. If these leaders have valid objections to any candidate he is not hired. This approach is built on the principle that from participation in decision-making and organized action comes citizen responsibility. As might be expected, there are many stresses and strains in the relationship between ACTION-Housing, a part of the urban establishment, and the independent citizen councils with which it has agreements. Strains will grow as the program grows. They can be a source of vitality.

At the beginning of 1963, three large Pittsburgh neighborhoods, from among several expressing interest, were chosen for a five-year test of the new approach. The department of city planning aided in the selection. Those chosen were Homewood-Brushton, Hazelwood-Glenwood, and Perry Hilltop. Between them they held almost seventy-five thousand people — one-eighth of the city's population. Homewood-Brushton was a declining middle-income, largely Negro area, with several urban problems and some slum pockets. The pilot program leading to urban extension had been carried out there. A full account of the effort in this neighborhood will be found in the next chapter.

Hazelwood-Glenwood was a central-city steel mill area with high unemployment, low educational level, predominantly white with some racial tension, a bleak shopping street, some handsome residential sections, but apparent mental and physical blight. Initiative in Hazelwood-Glenwood had come from Father Joseph Meenan, a Catholic priest who began pulling leaders together in 1962 to plan a renewal effort. The group's first move was to ask assistance from ACTION-Housing. In those days the group was hard put to get ten people to a meeting. In late 1964, Father Meenan and the Hazelwood-Glenwood Urban Extension Council ran a community development education seminar five nights in a row with more than five hundred present every night.

Aided by the leadership of Robert B. Williams, a neighborhood extension worker who came out of the Peace Corps, the people of this neighborhood have pioneered the war on poverty by tackling their employment problems in depth. They have registered the unemployed, recruited and trained volunteer counsellors, guided hundreds into jobs or training programs. When they found no government courses available for some of their uneducated, low-skill registrants, they set up their own course in the neighborhood's Hungarian Social Hall, trained nineteen persons for hospital work, and helped seventeen of these obtain jobs in nearby hospitals.

Council committees are working with public and private resources to make a long-range social and physical renewal plan, to improve dilapidated housing, to support school improvements, to have new houses built on vacant hillsides, to open the industrial riverfront for boating, to modernize the business strip, publish a newspaper, and organize all residents into block groups. Tutoring programs are run for children who are not doing well in school. Racial tensions are eased by Negro and white working together on committees. Courses in effective management have been set up in the neighborhood by Duquesne University for local merchants and a modern recreation demonstration is under way, although these two programs have run into many difficulties.

The third neighborhood chosen was Perry Hilltop, an outlying, nearly all-white, middle-class area in sound condition, with decline at the edges, where the largest problem was apathy. The strategy in Perry Hilltop has been to improve public services sharply so that the present sound elements of the neighborhood can be preserved, with more modern public facilities, a community spirit, and good race relations established in the process.

Staff leadership here has been furnished by David Herlinger, a former insurance salesman who has shifted his career to urban affairs, and Johanna Cocheres, a Perry Hilltop housewife long active in PTA and neighborhood affairs who had been a schoolteacher before marriage and who is now set to make a new career of neighborhood development.

The making of the city's first comprehensive neighborhood public service plan has been undertaken by this area's citizen organization, the Perry Hilltop Action Council. In this effort, the Council is aided by the Institute of Local Government of the University of Pittsburgh, and by city government. City hall's cooperation, which came reluctantly, is courageous. The planning is very likely to result in criticism and pressure for city hall, even as it devises new, improved methods of neighborhood traffic control, garbage pickup, street maintenance, and the like.

Teams of citizens, university consultants, and public officials are examining every Perry Hilltop street, laying out new widenings, openings, and extensions. They are evaluating lighting, fire and police protection, schools, parks, and playgrounds. The area has a magnificent 250-acre, largely undeveloped park, for which they are creating a complete development plan. They are learning about new, efficient methods for routine housekeeping tasks like sewer cleaning. Hopefully, they will come up with ideas valuable to the whole city.

In explaining further the thought behind neighborhood urban extension, ACTION-Housing's Loshbough paraphrases the words of Douglas Ensminger, the Ford Foundation's representative in India, with whom he worked on India's community development program for several years:

Extension starts with a point of view about people. It is aimed at helping people help themselves. Extension in a neighborhood begins with needs of people, as they see them, or as they come to see them as education takes hold. Extension moves from the recognized problem, to a desire to do something about it, to an understanding of what caused the problem, to an understanding of what might be done to improve the condition, to a desire to take the necessary action, to taking the action. Finally, with the necessary action taken and satisfaction derived from the new ways of thinking and doing, these new ways replace the old.

The effort in each of the three neighborhoods seeks to enroll citizens regardless of status — rich, middle-income, and poor — in accordance with the extension principle that the talents of all are important to the building of the city. This has not been easy for apathy is heavy in all such areas. Citizen fund raising, for instance, has not been fully successful in any one of the three neighborhoods.

Neighborhood urban extension follows the principle that the basic key to urban vigor lies in the conversion of the mass of apathetic urban dwellers into a fully participating citizenry, taking responsibility for their own environment — physical, economic, and social. Pittsburgh's anti-poverty program, under the direction of the Mayor's Committee on Human Resources, Inc., is being modelled on this approach, with ACTION-Housing carrying out a large part of the program under contract to the Mayor's Committee.

\* \* \*

Each approach described in this chapter seeks to find a process — a method of urban community organization — effective enough to transform declining urban living areas into strong modern neighborhood communities. No one of the approaches has yet been applied to a troubled suburb, but this probably will happen soon for there are now many troubled suburbs.

There is much to be learned from the experiences gained by participants in all four of the approaches that have been discussed in this chapter. No one of them has yet proven itself a success, but each has achieved enough to warrant further demonstration and support.

In New York City, city government with its massive services is firmly committed to helping older neighborhoods and to bringing services closer to the people through local city halls. It seeks to hand over increased responsibility to citizens as a neighborhood conservation program develops.

The Industrial Areas Foundation stirs the revolutionary spirit in deprived neighborhood people and helps them form power organizations capable of getting what they need. IAF's approach seeks to build a self-sufficient and self-reliant community, with needed services provided by neighborhood people themselves or obtained by demands upon government. It rejects any close, cooperative relationship with government. In Chicago's Woodlawn Negro solidarity seems to be one of the unifying factors of the IAF effort, but a factor which tends to harden the area in its segregation and lessen its chances of eventually achieving the integration necessary for maximum neighborhood development.

The social invention organizations in Boston, New Haven, Oakland, and elsewhere are instruments seeking to improve the urban establishment from within. They offer citizens, particularly deprived ones, support in meeting their needs, thereby making possible change without revolution. They seek to modernize services through the direction of experts. The participation of citizens is as receivers rather than partners, and consequently there is not full opportunity to develop sense of community through joint decision-making. Some of the new and modernized neighborhood institutions, however, like community schools and employment centers, can contribute substantially to such a sense.

Fundamental differences between the IAF and social invention approach can be seen in this quote from Paul Ylvisaker: ". . . it is our belief that a middle ground of constructive action must be maintained and continually widened if the causes of protest are to be removed, and if protest itself is to become more than a social irritant and an invitation to violence. It is also our belief that seemingly incompatible interests can be reconciled and seemingly impossible problems can be resolved if they are subjected to reason, ingenuity, and experimentation."

Charles Silberman, in his provocative book, *Crisis in Black and White,* compares the two approaches in detail and concludes that the IAF approach is effective because it changes people by giving them responsibility and dignity, while the social invention approach is relatively ineffective because it is paternalistic. The social invention approach cannot be swept aside quite this easily, however, because in many places it is getting concrete results. The school system in New Haven is becoming a better one. The Boston neighborhoods are getting better employment services, Oakland is meeting its problems of migrant multi-problem families and delinquency in schools.

Neighborhood urban extension seeks to create initiative in neighborhood people for revolutionary changes, and then to achieve these changes through self-help and cooperative links to the urban establishment. Needed services are planned for and sought with the neighborhood people working cooperatively but firmly with city government and other resources. When all else fails neighborhood urban extension uses militant action. For instance, when the state government delayed endlessly in construction of a long-promised new bridge linking Hazelwood-Glenwood with neighboring communities, citizens blockaded the old bridge until they were promised a date on which construction would begin.

This Pittsburgh approach seeks to build a sense of community not only within the neighborhood but between the neighborhood and other neighborhoods with which it cooperates in joint efforts (such as a program to remove abandoned cars) and with the whole metropolis. Progress is made in integration because white and Negro plan and act together on neighborhood problems. But so far little has been done in any of the three Pittsburgh neighborhoods to include integration as a consciously sought goal in long-range planning.

IAF and neighborhood urban extension put their emphasis on neighborhood leadership determining its own goals. New York's neighborhood conservation and the social invention organizations put emphasis on effective new services to aid neighborhood people, with goals determined largely from the top.

*    *    *

The responsible citizen is the basic ingredient in neighborhood development. He is both the chief agent for achieving improvement and the chief client to benefit from improvement. When the citizen plans and acts he becomes a man of dignity. The effort to be undertaken is so complex, however, he needs an ally in the person of the professional neighborhood worker. A key element in all approaches is this trained neighborhood professional. Probably no large urban effort can go far without his leadership. The tendency is to have more and more of such professionals recruited from the neighborhoods and trained on the job.

This ally is not a city planner, a social worker, a political action man, or any other specialist. He is an all-around man in urban neighborhood affairs who knows how and where to find the specialists when they are needed. He is a warm, imaginative, dedicated man (or woman) who works with and through neighborhood people to help them build a strong local community. He can help unite people and police in a campaign to achieve safe streets; people, teachers, and the education department of a local university to achieve quality schools; people and the state employment service to place all of the neighborhood's unemployed into retraining and jobs; people and planners toward thinking out the future of the neighborhood.

In Hyde Park-Kenwood, neighborhood professionals were recruited and paid for by neighborhood residents and institutions. In the urban extension neighborhoods of Pittsburgh this cost has been met by national and local foundations, by corporations, the Community Chest, and neighborhood people themselves. In Woodlawn a national community-organization foundation, two church denominations and neighborhood people contributed the necessary amount. In New Haven and Boston national and local foundations gave the money; in New York City, it was supplied by city government and neighborhood sponsors. In some other places the neighborhood professional is provided by urban renewal authorities, school boards, health departments, universities, civic organizations, community chests, and settlement houses.

The minimum cost of neighborhood office and staff is about fifty cents per year for each person in the area. Homewood-Brushton, for example, has thirty thousand people and the budget during its first three years was a modest $15,000 per year. No concerned citizens, however, should ever hold back a spontaneous development effort because they do not have a professional staff. The history of neighborhood efforts like those in Hyde Park-Kenwood, Hazelwood-Glenwood, and elsewhere, is that citizens can initiate much on their own, and find a source of professional help as their effort grows, and as they really need it.

Funds from the federal government's war on poverty now are available to pay for such professionals for revitalization programs in low-income neighborhoods. Hopefully in many urban places poverty funds are going to be imaginatively employed to create new and better approaches to the making of strong and vital neighborhoods. Demonstration projects in juvenile delinquency prevention and manpower retraining, financed by federal grants, are now under way in more than 100 cities. Out of these are already coming some additional significant approaches, for many of them involve quite comprehensive neighborhood development programs.

There is some tendency for neighborhood development approaches to become alike as they are applied to problems and opportunities whose roots are similar in all urban places. But since neighborhoods and their needs vary widely, in spite of the similarity of problems, it is important that a spirit of innovation and experiment be kept alive in each approach. Further pressure for them to become alike results from the fact that all of them are drawing more and more funds from the same federal programs which are governed by the same standards. The tendency is for the militant "fight city hall" approach to become less militant and closer to the establishment (as witness there is the history of the Back of the Yards Council whose leaders now serve on boards and commissions of city government), and for the establishment-sponsored approach to move closer to the people.

Any promising new approaches — along with the four discussed in this chapter — should be given full opportunity to demonstrate the effectiveness of their different techniques. Living areas exist in endless variety. A variety of approaches is needed to achieve strong neighborhood communities everywhere.

# Chapter 9

# HOMEWOOD-BRUSHTON: A NEW APPROACH AT WORK

February 17, 1964, was a historic day for the Homewood-Brushton neighborhood of Pittsburgh. Three hundred citizens went before the city council to present a plan for the future of their neighborhood. This plan looked ahead to drastic rearrangement of streets, enlargement of an industrial area, tearing down of obsolete buildings, construction of new housing, expansion of schools, and a host of other renewal actions. These proud citizens had initiated the plan and raised funds to help pay for it. Much of it had been shaped by their ideas, for they had worked intimately, step by step, with professional planners to help produce it. The plan was unanimously accepted by the council, and became part of the official plan of the city.

Since that day, the pace of modernization has stepped up greatly in the gray area that is Homewood-Brushton. It is of district neighborhood size with central shopping center, churches and schools, and thirty thousand people — enough to attract political attention. Teams of technical specialists have been sitting down with homeowners to work out ways to make their old houses livable and modern. A site has been selected for a new school. Three small playgrounds have been built. New stores have opened. A neighborhood employment center has been started. Home day-care service has been launched to aid mothers who must work. Three neighborhood industrial plants have been helped to expand. Zoning chaos has ended and better future use of neighborhood land assured. This self-help plan has given force and guidance to the joint efforts of local people and has provided city-wide resources to transform Homewood-Brushton into a modern urban neighborhood.

Homewood-Brushton is the story of neighborhood urban extension in operation. The full story goes back many years prior to the February date. When the Civil War ended, Homewood-Brushton was a mile-and-a-half-square tract of farmland east of Pittsburgh that was being carved into handsome estates. The focal point of the settlement was the Homewood stop of the Pennsylvania Railroad, whose main line cut through the area then as it does today. A fashionable race track was operated north of the railroad station.

Homewood-Brushton was annexed to Pittsburgh in 1868, but maintained its suburban character for many years. Change to a city neighborhood came in slow, easy stages. Electric trolley lines were extended out into Homewood-Brushton from the center of Pittsburgh in 1892-93. Small homes were built and population boomed as moderate income families moved in. By 1920 many of the large estates had become sites for industrial plants or for groups of small houses. Numerous, closely packed two-and-a-half-story houses replaced the race track. A massive wall of trolley barns was built in the heart of the neighborhood. (Today it is Homewood-Brushton's single largest physical problem. The plan calls for replacing it with new housing.)

Until the end of World War I, Homewood-Brushton was marked by growth and construction; then gradual decline began. The remaining large homes had aged. Most of their original owners were gone. Some of these old mansions were subdivided into apartments. Population gradually became a mixture of laborers, craftsmen, white-collar workers, and professionals — Negro as well as white. During the Great Depression some of the small houses began to hold a second or even a third family. This process of subdividing was accelerated by the housing shortage of World War II. Homewood-Brushton entered the 1950's with all the marks of a gray area: overcrowding, rising crime rate, heavy traffic on residential streets, a shortage of recreational facilities, empty stores, housing in need of repair, inadequate schools, insufficient public services, and low morale — all compounded by rapid racial transition.

Some Negroes had lived in Homewood-Brushton as early as 1870. The number grew slowly, up to 1930, when Negroes were 11 percent of the population. They were 13 percent in 1940, 22 percent in 1950, and by 1960 soared to 66 percent. Today the neighborhood is almost a Negro ghetto. Negro families purchasing houses in Homewood-Brushton in the 1950's were struggling people, buying their first homes, and proud of their new status. They took to community activity with the same gusto and hope as new suburbanites. In 1954, these newcomers began to join with some of the old-time Negro residents to form block clubs. The clubs united into the Homewood Community Improvement Association.

They reported housing violations, held contests to promote beautiful yards, sought increased police protection, and fought to halt an increase in taverns. Many small successes were achieved, and the clubs began to push for some larger needs, like new streets, recreation facilities, removal of empty, dilapidated buildings, increased off-street parking, a new school, employment services, and other things that can help rehabilitate a down-at-the-heels neighborhood. Pressure was put on city government and downtown civic agencies. ACTION-Housing, the Health and Welfare Association, and the mayor's office responded. Surveys were made. These showed that Homewood-Brushton was a sound area capable of being modernized.

Merchants and factory managers from the neighborhood were brought together with block-club leaders, clergymen, and school principals to form a new organization to work with the downtown resources. Called the Homewood-Brushton Citizens Renewal Council, the new organization got off to an impressive start. The mayor addressed a kickoff dinner on February 9, 1960. Ambitious statements were made. Television cameras whirred. Flashbulbs popped. For one day, Homewood-Brushton was front-page news. The morning after dawned with a small steering committee trying to lay hold of a few large, difficult, and unglamorous problems.

With advice and guidance from its downtown allies, the committee moved, haltingly, to some fundamental things. It chose to affiliate with ACTION-Housing for sustained staff assistance. It raised $10,200 in the neighborhood from industry, merchants, and residents to help finance the plan, and made arrangements with the city planning department and the Health and Welfare Association to furnish planners. It established a committee of citizens to work with the planners.

Through ACTION-Housing, it obtained a $45,000 grant from the Buhl Foundation of Pittsburgh to help underwrite a neighborhood office and staff. It secured the assistance of the city health department in beginning a door-to-door home improvement campaign. It held twice-monthly meetings with the heads of downtown agencies, including the school superintendent and the mayor's urban renewal coordinator, to explore ways the neighborhood could be aided.

On September 1, 1960, the program was formally under way; in operation were a full-time organizer supplied by ACTION-Housing (the neighborhood extension worker), an office with a secretary, a full-time city planner, and many citizens who had become involved through membership on newly established committees. The three elements for a strong neighborhood renewal effort had come together: neighborhood people, full-time professional staff, and the resources of the city.

The new organization sought to do three things. First, find and develop a large number of neighborhood leaders; second, develop a strong, long-range plan; three, solve certain short-range problems right away. The philosophy of this program from the beginning was one of maximum self-help — people acquiring skills, acting for themselves and for their neighborhood, using their own efforts but also utilizing the governments, corporations, and organizations of the whole metropolis, and learning from the neighborhood extension worker. Through this broadened concept of self-help the organization has sought to build enlightened, responsible citizen-leaders able to work effectively with the private and public power of all Pittsburgh.

During 1961 the organization's temporary steering committee was replaced by a senate of two hundred members, a board of directors, and an executive committee. The senate was created as the basic policy-making group. It is made up of block-club presidents, members elected at-large, merchants and industrialists, and one representative of each church, club, or other organized group. It meets quarterly to make basic policy. The board of directors is made up of twenty-one members elected by the senate plus all chairmen of standing committees. Meeting monthly, it oversees the running of the organization. A large majority of the members of both the senate and board are Negroes and residents of the neighborhood.

More than five hundred people in Homewood-Brushton have assumed some definite responsibility for carry-

ing on the program. The degree of their involvement has
varied widely. Slowly, but surely, the Council has developed a large corps of trained people able to deal seriously and responsibly with nearly every neighborhood
problem and opportunity.

An example will illustrate this. The education committee, early in the program, studied the overcrowding
of public schools which resulted as white families with
children attending Catholic schools left the neighborhood,
to be replaced by Negro families whose children attended
public schools. The need for more classrooms was acute.
In view of the long-range planning going on, which would
determine the best sites for permanent new schools,
immediate attention was given to some sensible stopgap
measures.

The committee worked with local school principals,
gathered facts, talked with PTA leaders and formulated
a three-step solution: (1) rent temporary space in existing church buildings; (2) construct demountable units
on existing school sites; (3) plan for one or two new
permanent schools. Church facilities were surveyed and
demountable requirements ascertained. Meetings were
held with both the staff and board members of the Board
of Public Education. The education committee found the
Board of Education staff formulating a scheme to buy
and restore, at great expense, an obsolete and empty
school building in the neighborhood. With facts, figures,
and a portrayal of neighborhood desires the committee
convinced the Board of Education in a series of mature
discussions to drop this scheme (it would have eliminated
the neighborhood's chance of obtaining a new school)
and persuaded the Board to adopt the committee's own
three-point plan.

Residents who participated directly during the early
years of the program were mainly the employed, stable,
middle-income, better-educated people of the neighbor-

hood. Only a handful of the thousands of unemployed, poverty-haunted, less stable, undereducated people of Homewood-Brushton have been involved. The council has since attempted to reach and recruit people in this group through such programs as an employment center, a housing clinic, preschool centers, and other services that meet immediate, concrete needs. With additional funds furnished through the war on poverty, employment and housing activities have been expanded, and involvement of low-income families has increased. Several low-income persons have become members of the council's Board of Directors.

A small monthly newspaper, underwritten by local merchants and distributed by volunteers, has been established by the council. Other media used to spread word of the neighborhood effort have been bulletin boards in stores, church bulletins, a local radio station, daily newspapers, the weekly, city-wide Negro newspaper. Effective distribution of information to the whole neighborhood — so crucial in an effort of this kind — is far from achieved. The key man in getting out information, finding leaders, and helping them unfold their talents has been the neighborhood extension worker, the full-time staff man supplied by ACTION-Housing.

In Homewood-Brushton this has been a rotund, energetic young Irishman named Kiernan Stenson. With his lively, tough mind putting forth imaginative ideas, he has moved night and day through the neighborhood, into homes, bars, church basements, and downtown to the agency offices. Tirelessly he has helped citizens and officials to catch the vision of a new Homewood-Brushton, and then recruited them to help achieve the vision. Patiently, but with strong initiative, he has helped citizens to develop their talents, take on responsibility, and begin to make decisions for themselves and their neighborhood. In early 1965, after 3½ years of creative staff leadership, Stenson became director of operations for Pittsburgh's Mayor's Committee on Human Resources, Inc., over-all war on poverty organization for the city.

Leaders like Mrs. Sarah Campbell have emerged. She is a housewife of conviction and drive who has headed the neighborhood's employment committee. With the dozen members of her committee, she has registered and interviewed a thousand unemployed residents in one year, and helped guide half of these into retraining courses or jobs. She has done so well she has been hired full-time to run the neighborhood employment center.

Typical entries in one of her weekly reports read:

Three mechanic trainees in about not receiving allowance checks. They were broke. Loaned one $5.00 to get some food for family and for carfare. Carfare for two others. I called to find out about checks. They will be mailed today.

Gave tests to ten applicants for service station courses. Some were petrified. We assured them these would not keep them out of class, were just for teacher to know more about them. Some of their buddies came along to see what was going on. A couple wanted to know if they could get in class; were surprised to learn how easy to apply. We signed them up. These two have been hanging in the pool hall for a year. Our trainees keep spreading the word and we're getting more of these lost guys.

Went to Tyson Metals Company to discuss job openings. Got to talk to two of the five Tyson brothers. Picked up two job orders. Back to office. Talked to a trainee from scientific-helper training course who has to write something on a medical subject for the class. I made an appointment for him with a local doctor so he could get some background. This boy never got by the tenth grade, but he was so excited you would think he was writing a thesis for a doctor's degree.

Another neighborhood leader is Roger Taliaferro, a

mailman who became chairman of the complaints committee. Each day he would finish his route about 3:30
in the afternoon and hurry to the council's small neighborhood office where he would stay for two hours, listen-
ing to stories of abandoned cars and plugged sewers from
fellow residents, calling about the complaints to the
various public officials he had come to know well, and
systematically getting small improvements made and city
services improved.

Hundreds of such leaders have come forth, and in
their common effort they have widened the sense of community in Homewood-Brushton. Many have worked on
the making of the long-range plan. Three dozen people
serving on planning committees came to see that a neighborhood in decline for more than forty years, suffering
from out-of-date houses and streets, from mixtures of
stores, factories, and homes on the same blocks, from
the tensions of racial panic and segregation, from all the
urban pressures of our time, is not revived and made
tranquil and handsome in a day — or a year. To find new
life, they realized, a neighborhood must plan ahead for
ten, twenty, or even thirty years.

As each step of the plan developed, it was reviewed
by the citizens' committees, and with individuals and
groups affected, including neighborhood business, industry, and institutions. There were many long, hard, sometimes bitter sessions. The planning committees, working
closely with professional planners, made recommendations to the executive board of the renewal council. A
number of suggestions involving traffic, school sites, industrial expansion, timing of clearance and construction,
treatment of hillsides, and other matters arising out of
these discussions were integrated by the planners into
the final proposals.

To reach the many block clubs, church organizations,
PTAs and other community groups a physical planner

trained a group of alert residents to become "communicators." These men and women went throughout the community explaining the proposals to their neighbors, gathering comments, questions, and criticism which were fed back to the planners. Here are excerpts from two reports of communicators.

From Communicator Robert Boulden:

There were a lot of questions at this meeting. How much notice will people get before they have to sell their homes? What kind of prices will be paid? Will new homes be built on some of the vacant hillsides first? Should people let their homes run down or keep them up?

There has been a lot of speculation, and a lot of rumors have passed around this block. A lot more work on getting people involved has to be done in this block.

From Communicator Richard M. Adams:

This group favorable to the plan. But wanted to know about some immediate matters, like how come the old Lang Hotel is allowed to exist in such condition? How do we get more Negroes working in Homewood plants? What about more parklets for small children? Will the saloons remain if the car barns are demolished? Will people who have to move get priority on the new houses?

President of this block club keeps it well informed. They really could have done without me. They approve the physical plan, and are more concerned about getting a social plan for unwed mothers, dropouts, school discipline and narcotics.

Mr. Boulden was a TV repairman and Mr. Adams a postal worker. Both have since started careers as neighborhood development workers.

There emerged from this long process a plan which

has in it the expressed needs of neighborhood people as well as the technical know-how of professional planners. The plan calls for eliminating housing in the industrial section and turning it into an expanded modern industrial park; shrinking, consolidating, modernizing the shopping section; building new housing on vacant hillsides; fixing up most existing housing; providing attractive and modern schools, play areas, and streets. The social part of the plan sets forth programs to solve problems of employment, family life, crime, health, and recreation. It will take at least twenty years and $20 million to carry out the full plan. The first $3½ million in urban renewal funds became available as soon as the plan was approved in 1964.

Taking a casual drive through Homewood-Brushton today, early 1965, one will not see a bright and shiny living area. To be sure, hundreds of new porches and painted house fronts can be seen (out of thousands), new playgrounds, two new parking lots, a dozen and a half bright new temporary schoolrooms, a few whole blocks with handsome landscaping and neat houses, some newly paved streets, new street-sweeping signs, mercury vapor lights on arterial streets, police patrolling with dogs, and a neighborhood employment center.

But the general appearance is still drab and run-down. There are unkempt houses, empty stores, abandoned cars, junk yards, bleak factories mixed with homes, blocks with little grass and no trees, unemployed men loitering. Conversation with residents met at random would reveal fear in many, despair in some from poverty and discrimination, and still quite a number without any knowledge of the renewal effort. A discussion with the renewal council leaders would bring forth a frank admission that the neighborhood is not yet meeting its time schedule for raising money so as to become financially independent of ACTION-Housing and able to pay its own staff. A strong determination to catch up would be expressed.

There would be revealed, also, a lack of decision on the question of restoring a racial balance. There are many views on this: some feel a racial balance is desirable but first full attention must be given to renewal; some say it makes no difference, the important thing is an orderly, attractive neighborhood; and others oppose a balance since it would reduce housing available to Negroes. One white official tells the ominous story of a Negro home-owner asking him, "What are you trying to do, make this neighborhood so nice we Negroes won't want to move out into white neighborhoods?" Homewood-Brushton, one of these years, may have all the qualities of a good neighborhood community — except integration.

Neighborhood leaders have strong, direct contact with the school superintendent, city councilmen, the mayor, and other decision makers. They freely make criticism of the urban establishment. But the neighborhood probably also needs an independent political arm of the kind that elected Abner Mikva.

A closer examination of the results of the neighborhood effort, however, would also reveal many not-so-visible results, including demolition of twenty-two empty buildings, preschool training classes for children from backward homes, removal of over one thousand abandoned cars, racial integration of the work force in several plants and stores, and correction of two thousand housing code defects.

The stage is ready for drastic physical and social change. This change is made inevitable by the force now generated by the leadership mobilized, the relationships built between white and Negro neighborhood leaders, the sound long-range plan, the links with downtown agencies, the vigorous professional staff, and the aggressive renewal council organization. Emerging slowly out of the gray is a modern new Homewood-Brushton.

# Chapter 10

## A NOTE OF CRITICISM

The effort to vitalize metropolis and its neighborhoods is one of the significant works of our age, pushed forward by thousands of dedicated professionals and volunteers. But this is not to say that all goes well with this complicated effort. Transformation of the living areas of America into attractive neighborhood communities which respect and promote the dignity of man is a crusade that has conflicts of interest, bumbling and muddling, and many mistakes, along with progress and occasional brilliant success.

It must be admitted that so far there have been more hopes than results. In Hyde Park-Kenwood, Homewood-Brushton, Northwood Acres and all the hundreds of other places with serious development efforts, work is long, hard, frustrating, and only beginning. Much is yet to be learned. There are blind alleys being explored and more ahead. There are problems barely touched.

One of the most important contributions that supporters of these efforts can make is to take an occasional hard, critical look at what is happening. No movement as large and as new as urban development can roll on without producing some methods that have flaws, some programs that are ineffective, and some results that are inadequate. Honest evaluation is not only good for the soul — it is good for the metropolis and all its neighborhoods. Robert Weaver himself, head of the federal government's urban development programs, has declared repeatedly, "Urban renewal is not, nor should it be, above criticism or re-examination."

The evaluation that follows centers on three major questions brought to the fore by recent development efforts:

1. Is the forced purchase of property in many neighborhoods causing undue hardship?

2. How good is the neighborhood environment created by development projects?

3. Are development efforts comprehensive enough?

The power of the government to purchase private property, whether the owner wants to sell or not, is known as eminent domain. It is a power that goes back to Roman Law and the Magna Carta. A guarantee that payment be made for such taking is spelled out in the Fifth Amendment to the Constitution, which states, ". . . nor shall private property be taken for public use without just compensation." Urban renewal cannot proceed without this power. When a slum section is to be torn down, it is necessary to purchase all the property in a fairly large area, otherwise the resulting piece of cleared land would not be suitable for rebuilding. Without the power of forced purchase, government would have to pay exorbitant prices in order to obtain all the needed property in an urban renewal neighborhood.

In applying the Fifth Amendment the courts have interpreted "just compensation" to mean fair-market value, and they have generally ruled that only tangible, see-and-feel property be paid for. This means that indirect losses — like a shopkeeper having half his customers relocate out of the neighborhood, or a man losing the convenience of living within walking distance of his work — are not compensated. Often in urban renewal project neighborhoods near universities or hospitals older people live in rented homes or large apartments, and sublet rooms to students or nurses. When forced to move, such people often lose their livelihood without full compensation. Even if they own their homes, and are paid for the real estate, they usually cannot find a property for the same price, which they can use in the same way. The Hyde Park-Kenwood small businessmen who quit business after dislocation were not compensated for the value of their lost business. They were paid only for their real estate and the equipment left behind, if any.

As the American Bar Association has pointed out, the rules of eminent domain were set down a long time ago, in a "bygone, comparatively uncomplicated age," when forced purchases were few and involved mostly vacant land. Now forced purchases are staggering in size and number. There are over seven hundred separate urban renewal agencies around the country with the power to acquire land. Sidney Z. Searles, in the *National Civic Review,* has estimated that in the ten years ending in 1973 these agencies will have cleared and sold two billion dollars' worth of property, five times the amount involved in all sales of publicly owned land between 1785 and 1956. In addition, the interstate highway program will, by 1972, take six billion dollars' worth of land — 730,000 separate pieces, on which live millions of people.

Furthermore, urban renewal and highway building are not the only development programs that take land. Programs for new schools, public housing, parking lots, parks, and other public purposes, often involve forced purchase. In one way or another forced purchase will affect nearly every neighborhood in the nation in the next ten years.

Like the businessman who loses all or part of his business without being compensated for the "good will" built up over years, families often suffer heavy losses when forced to give up a house. The price paid a family may cover the market value of their home, but be far too little to buy a house of comparable size and comfort in another neighborhood. Or a family may have an apartment that rents for $75, and be unable to find a comparable one for less than $100 in any other neighborhood.

Then there are human values, family roots, and ties to a local community. The family that has been in the same house forty years and has put down deep roots is compensated the same as a newcomer family that has been in a house six months. There is _o compensation for the deep human loss that comes with being torn apart from friends, familiar neighborhood, parish church, and a community.

Urban renewal is finding public support harder to come by. And no wonder. There are too many hardships to too many people. Real estate developers benefit. City tax coffers benefit. Businessmen and residents who remain in a renewal area often have an improved environment. Universities and hospitals buying cleared land benefit. But there are some businessmen and families forced to move who suffer economic and psychological hardship.

The "some" should be emphasized. Among the businessmen and families forced to move from a project area, there are always those who gain. Some free themselves from property they have long wanted to dispose of and could find no buyer for. Some businessmen find themselves doing twice the business at their new locations. Some renters are helped to become owners while being relocated. There are numerous instances of gains. Perhaps more gain than lose. The fact remains, however, that many suffer. And this is unjust and largely unnecessary. In time it could make urban renewal politically impossible. This would be tragic, because urban renewal is an indispensable tool for the proper development of the metropolis and its neighborhoods. But its burden should be supported by the whole of society, not just by those who by accident happen to be in the way.

The payment of full compensation — to cover intangible as well as tangible losses and to make possible the purchase of equal replacement housing elsewhere at no increased expense to the relocatee — seems only basic justice. And it would help the neighborhoods into which relocatees move. If a relocated family comes into a new neighborhood with adequate funds to buy or rent a decent home and to maintain it well, the new neighborhood is helped. If the family's resources are not adequate and it is forced to crowd into second-rate housing or into good housing it cannot afford to maintain, then the new neighborhood is harmed. Full compensation could be paid in several ways. It could be an outright lump payment, or some kind of monthly housing payment, or a combination of these. The important matter is that the relocated family end up in good housing in a good neighborhood, and that it do so as a matter of right, for hardship suffered on behalf of society, and not as a matter of charity.

Changes in the laws governing urban renewal would be needed to achieve such a goal. The 1964 Housing Act took small steps toward doing this, by providing rent supplements for some low-income families forced to move. A measure to compensate small businessmen for business losses caused by moving was defeated, but in time such a measure will pass. Full compensation should apply to those who lose a business as well as those who lose a home.

Full compensation would mean that if a druggist made $10,000 a year, and after relocation could make only $5,000 for the first two years while building up a new trade, he would be compensated for the difference. It would mean that a family living in a seven-room home close to stores, transportation, and church, whose home was only worth $9,000 in the regular real estate market, would nevertheless be paid $12,000 if it would cost them $12,000 to buy a comparable house in a comparable location elsewhere. A family renting for $75 and only able to find a comparable apartment at $100 would be compensated for the difference.

Such broadened legislation would enable small businessmen and families caught up in forced purchase to benefit as do most other affected interests. The compensation should be paid in full at the time of the taking of the property; the dislocated should not have to wait while administrative or court procedures drag on. Delay in payment works a particular hardship on those homeowners who find themselves evicted from their old house without money to buy a new one. And perhaps a way must be found to compensate for an intangible like community roots — say by awarding residents an extra $100 for every five years they have been in their old dwelling place.

Hardships can also be kept down by decreasing the number of buildings demolished in a renewal neighborhood, and increasing the number repaired and modernized. Many times buildings are owned by families of modest means, who cannot afford to modernize. Since the results of renewal benefit the common good, there probably should be a direct subsidy given to owners in renewal areas so they can improve their homes and bring them up to good standards. By increasing fix-up of homes and stores, and cutting down on demolition, community roots in neighborhoods can be preserved.

Ralph McGill, publisher of the *Atlanta Constitution,* has written:

> Two of the reasons slum dwellers have resented and resisted urban renewal is that they possess a sense of neighborhood where they live and know that

the new housing would not be really available for them because of cost. Their community feeling may have been built merely around a neighboring tavern and delicatessen, but they knew these places and were known by their neighbors.

Justice is the first consideration here. But also at stake is the future of renewal efforts. Large-scale government programs will be in political danger if the thousands now suffering hardship turn into millions in the years ahead.

Another test of the success of urban development and all of its works is its effects on man, which brings us to the second question. What kind of environment is urban development producing? There is no simple answer.

Urban renewal has moved slowly. In fifteen years, 1700 projects have been conceived and scheduled in over seven hundred towns, suburbs, and cities. Less than half have actually gotten under way, and only about one hundred have been completed. In many places land cleared by urban renewal has lain idle for years without anyone taking much interest in building on it.

On the private development side, twenty million new homes have been built in the suburbs since the war, and sold mostly to middle-income families, a prodigious achievement. Yet, we must admit these homes have gone up largely in monotonous tracts, with inadequate inside space, and segregated inhabitants — factors which make the building of community spirit difficult.

As urban development has gone forward since 1949, segregation by race has intensified within the city's neighborhoods and Negroes have not yet been able to move into the suburbs in any numbers. The relocation that has been part of urban development has definitely contributed to this apartheid pattern. A great opportunity has been missed here — and a greater one is still before us — to use relocation as a tool for promoting neighborhood integration. The control that public agencies can exercise over population movement through relocation could make possible real progress toward integrated neighborhoods. Some officials are already predicting that by the end of the sixties it will be federal policy, and local policy in many cities, forthrightly to use relocation to move Negroes into white neighborhoods.

The twin tragedies of intensified segregation and urban ugliness merge in a monstrous mistake like Chicago's massive wall of Negro public housing which runs unbroken for five miles along the city's new Dan Ryan Expressway. Such ghettos are rigid class islands which break the metropolis apart, destroy its sense of community. Massive public housing projects are not neighborhoods but compounds. They are in part the result of federal economic limitations, and of a fruitless social-planning notion that an antiseptic physical environment can solve all of a family's problems. Often such projects result from a political decision: most voters and officials have rejected the poor, and particularly the poor Negro, and they want them living apart.

Public housing should be woven into existing neighborhoods, with one promising method being the purchase and modernizing of existing housing as is being done in Philadelphia. This method provides a much more normal environment for the low-income family, and at the same time improves the neighborhood by modernizing some of its old housing. Legislative changes proposed in the 1965 Housing Bill could make this possible on a large scale.

Beauty is important in urban development. A nation as rich as ours, engaged in massive building and rebuilding efforts, should be greatly concerned with design, for the appearance of today's construction will for generations affect the spirit of man, whether it be public housing, shopping centers, or other new construction. The esthetic results of urban development are a matter of controversy and personal taste, and history will give the final verdict. It can be rather safely predicted, however, that much of today's work will be damned for its ugliness.

In 1963 an awards committee of the City Club of New York looked at the best new public buildings constructed during the previous five years, and decided not one was worthy of citation for excellence of design.

The Urban Renewal Administration has taken cognizance of this matter, and issued a policy statement which says, "urban renewal provides an unprecedented opportunity to rebuild major parts of our cities. Well designed, these can become assets — functionally and esthetically. But if these areas are poorly designed, rebuilt in uninteresting and unproductive patterns, a basic purpose for the expenditure of public funds and public effort will be lost."

Beauty is not just for downtown, the civic center, and a few other spectacular high points of a city. It is for everywhere; and very much for the neighborhood. It is to be seen in the fresh, modern town houses set amid the older buildings in Hyde Park-Kenwood (next to some rather ugly new high-rise buildings); in the restored town houses of Boston's Beacon Hill and New Haven's Wooster Square; and in the rebuilt "village" shopping street in Pittsburgh's Shadyside neighborhood. There is handsomeness in the designs for the several neighborhoods of Reston, Virginia, a whole new town being built within the Washington, D.C., metropolis. The restored white hill-houses of several San Francisco living areas, or the neat renewal homes of St. Louis' Cherokee neighborhood, are other good examples of attractiveness springing out of urban development efforts.

Since urban beauty is a result of human creation, probably the best way to seek it is that suggested by Martin Meyerson and Edward C. Banfield, two of the nation's leading students of urban affairs. They have suggested: "Certainly, all public buildings, even the most routine and out-of-the-way, ought to be regarded as opportunities for great architectural achievement. This means that the city must seek out great (but not necessarily famous) architects and give them the freedom, not only in essentials but in details as well, without which great art is impossible." The same can be done for parks and streets and private buildings and neighborhood shopping centers that are being remodeled. Good planners and good architects must be utilized for design and redesign.

Neighbors on a street can attain beauty together by choosing paint colors with care and advice. (There must be twenty-five thousand front porches in Pittsburgh painted an ugly and unnecessary dark green.) The householder can attain beauty by spending a little extra for a good architect when he modernizes his home. Sometimes the architect can save an owner more than his fee by his superior knowledge of materials, building methods, and contractor relations. When home modernization is carried out in an urban renewal area some free architectural services are usually available to homeowners.

Let creative men be given the freedom to ply their arts in urban development — then we need not fear the judgment of history. It may be that we are asking too much too soon from a movement that is young and faces enormous challenges from urban growth and decline. But we must ask much of it or the final result for man in metropolis will be miserable living areas.

In some ways the difficulty has been that the urban development effort has not yet quite become a movement, but is too much a scattering of projects and unconnected bits and pieces of effort with many gaps. Urban renewal, particularly, has proceeded project by project, without much real over-all planning to guide it. Expressways of magnificent size have crisscrossed through every metropolis but they do not always turn out to be in the right place. They often cut living areas apart, flood cars into small streets, block vistas, and produce new ugliness. The numerous little governments in each metropolis do not always cooperate. Where united efforts on refuse disposal, water supply, high schools, policing, support for cultural facilities, and the like, would greatly improve a living environment, there is often a selfish inaction.

Our third question concerns the comprehensiveness of neighborhood renewal efforts. Since 1949 the federal government has made vast funds available to cities for the physical renewal of worn-out areas, in the belief that a new physical environment could cure most of a city's problems and give it vitality. As Hyde Park-Kenwood learned, physical renewal is not enough. Rather there is needed a much more comprehensive planning and action effort. Homewood-Brushton has made strides toward this with its complete social plan. But even in that case, there are areas of neighborhood life — communications, economic strength — which have been insufficiently treated.

Physical regeneration of cities is essential to their development as places good for human life. Urban renewal is an indispensable process in this regeneration. It does not, by itself, however, mount the kind of attack that can stamp out the social problems in our cities. The festering seriousness of these social problems has been forced into the open by the marches and picketing of the Negro war of protest, by rent strikes, and by the violence of youth who are out of work and out of patience with society.

Realization that physical urban renewal is only half an answer for the needs of urban people has reached the White House and the Congress, and has resulted in the war on poverty, and civil rights legislation. The war on poverty is aimed directly at removing the causes of social disorder among families, and at bringing people out of poverty and into the mainstream of American life. It does not seek to make them comfortable in their poverty.

It makes possible drastic and comprehensive neighborhood social planning and action, as urban renewal makes possible drastic and comprehensive neighborhood physical planning and action. It is a joint effort of federal government and cities. There is heavy emphasis on the development of children and youth, in an attempt to break the cycle of poverty which runs from parents to children to grandchildren in some families.

The war on poverty is being carried out in the city streets by city people, with the federal government providing only money and advice. Local initiative determines what and how much is done. The war is just beginning. Whether its youth programs can motivate and train dropouts for modern occupations and place them in permanent jobs remains to be seen. Whether imaginative programs in health, housing, employment, education, and family growth can be devised by cities to solve problems that have eluded solution by past efforts likewise is a large question. Great opportunity is with us.

The war on poverty combined with urban renewal and other tools can make possible the comprehensive effort needed to revitalize low-income living areas. It will have little effect on the vast majority of middle-income areas where most of the people of metropolis now reside. These living areas can obtain most of what they need to carry out social and economic renewal through existing school systems, health, welfare and recreation agencies, health departments, churches, universities, and the like. But it takes initiative to go after these resources, courage to raise the money to pay for them, and careful planning to use them well.

The quality of urban neighborhood improvement efforts in the next twenty years will have profound effects on the lives of all of us. So far, the living environment resulting from such efforts is not all we expect. Well-serviced neighborhoods will result only from comprehensive planning and action. There has been little such planning and action actually carried out to date.

# Chapter 11

## EMERGING ALLIES: CHURCH AND UNIVERSITY

The new efforts to create modern neighborhoods are aimed at civilizing the urban place; the hope is to create living areas of justice, beauty, tranquility, prosperity, and human growth — a goal so bold and so broad that it will be realized only with total involvement of urban assets.

In the past, the work of civilizing cities has been left largely to local government and a few charitable and civic organizations. Now we are beyond this. In the first place local government has never been quite able to do the job by itself, even with civic supporters. In the second place, the urban settlement in our time has become so immense and complicated that local government alone is overwhelmed, especially in the metropolis, which is fragmented into many separate, jealous, noncooperative governments.

Today urban development requires a magnitude of effort beyond anything conceived in the past. The scale of money, power, human effort, and ideas now needed to vitalize urban neighborhoods and make possible a cohesive community is so great that every urban resource must be mobilized. Two of the most important, most powerful resources, with the deepest community roots, are the urban church and the urban university. Yet up until very recently they have been somewhat aloof from the physical and social environment around them. Now this is changing, as it must.

The change is most dramatically seen in the dedicated

171

outpouring of students, professors, and clergymen who have joined in the civil rights marches across the nation, especially in Mississippi and Alabama. This has happened with courage and sacrifice, and has done much to make the Negro protest movement effective. In the fundamental work of making an urban environment where Negro and white alike can find dignity Church and university have enormous opportunity to contribute.

The Church is becoming concerned with the urban environment in a variety of ways. During the 1950's, for instance, the Catholic Archdiocese of Chicago launched a fierce attack against the Hyde Park-Kenwood plan, charging that it would destroy too many sound buildings and dislocate too many poor families. While these charges were made without full understanding of the vast, complicated Hyde Park-Kenwood project, they did serve to shake up the thinking of Chicagoans about urban problems, brought on a great public debate in newspapers and city council chambers, and helped to break through the indifference of many citizens. In serving these purposes, the archdiocese played a valuable role and probably a proper one for the Church, in spite of the fact some of its charges were out of keeping with technical and sociological reality.

Probably the greatest contribution the Church has to make to the renewal of metropolis and the development of virile neighborhoods is in helping to create and strengthen a sense of community — that fragile, intangible something that binds people of all races, incomes, and religions in an area together in respect, dedication, love, mutual aid, responsibility. It is a thing of the mind and spirit — invisible and almost undefinable — and it is the element without which men do not live together in tranquility. The Church, in its most crucial mission, by its very nature, is concerned with creating a community of men under God. Nowhere is it better organized to do this than in the neighborhood.

When decay and disorder begin to swallow up an urban neighborhood, local churches face a question of survival and the challenge of a new mission. Churches that are courageous and imaginative in meeting change, are able to serve well people who need them more than ever. Churches that cling to the old order lose their relevance in men's lives. The old city churches that flee the urban rush of new people fail the challenge just as do those that stay and build walls around themselves.

The challenge is being met in many city neighborhoods. Pittsburgh's aging Hazelwood-Glenwood, depressed steel-mill neighborhood, is taking on new hope because of its grass-roots planning and renewal action program initiated by lay leadership of St. Stephen's Parish, with stimulation and strong support from the pastor. These churchmen have taken the cross of race tension and unemployment on themselves. On New York City's East Seventh Street, an old area which has been undergoing a spontaneous renovation, the Christian Missionary Church has worked with residents to create the Seventh Street Betterment Association. This association seeks to force landlords to repair tenement apartments, to find a recreation center for the numerous children who have no place to play, and to help bring a community pride to the street. (Residents have even contributed to have some trees planted at $117 each.) The Hyde Park-Kenwood effort began in 1949 at the initiative of lay and clerical leaders of three neighborhood churches: 57th Street Meeting of Friends (Quakers), First Unitarian Church, and KAM Temple.

In the North Washington section of the nation's capital, the pastor of Brightwood Park Methodist Church was one of a small group of community leaders who took the initiative in forming Neighbors, Inc. This organization has worked to maintain stability and harmony in a racially changing neighborhood. The present board of Neighbors, Inc., also includes the pastors of the local Presbyterian and Catholic churches, and the rabbi from the temple. East Baltimore Station Methodist Church and its pastor organized the South East Council for Community Services in an aging Baltimore neighborhood. This council has sought to push ahead social and physical planning.

Revitalization projects with the best long-range chance for success are proving to be those which unite all neighborhood forces — Negro and white; citizen and public official; businessman and worker; owner and tenant; Protestant, Jew and Catholic in one strong effort. Some neighborhood development efforts have been weakened and drained of effectiveness by exclusiveness, prejudice, and antagonism. Church leadership can help prevent this. No matter who originally initiates a neighborhood renewal effort, the program becomes strong as it becomes a community effort shared in by all interests, open to all institutions and individuals, and dominated by none.

Any parish church taking the initiative to start a program in its neighborhood finds it can usually obtain help from universities, redevelopment authorities, planning commissions, civic agencies, welfare councils, and a host of other forces. The first step in the Hazelwood-Glenwood program, for example, was making a balance sheet of neighborhood assets and liabilities, with the Sociology Department of Duquesne University assisting citizens to do this. It is the Church's responsibility, not to perform the work of development, but to arouse persons and institutions to do it. The place for the Church today is out in the streets, making its message relevant for urban man by knowing and understanding and dealing with the real problems of city and suburb. The Church has little meaning to man, and is little help to him, unless it understands the contemporary age and the human environment and needs that go with that age. It can only really do this by emersing itself completely in contemporary life, becoming part of it, living it.

In an earlier period of American life, fifty to eighty years ago, before the existence of the metropolis, when the large central city was coming into being amidst much agony, churches responded strongly to the human needs of the day. They took the lead in battling for better working and living conditions for the immigrants who poured into American cities from Europe. They created ethnic communities to protect and nurture the newcomers, and they fought (with only partial success) to improve the organization of municipal government so it could more effectively serve those who lived in cities. In those earlier years churches and churchmen were active in the settlement house movement, in tenement house reform, in combating religious and national prejudice, in helping to eradicate the evils of child labor, the exploitation of women, and sweatshop industry.

Robert Weaver, the scholarly Negro who has headed the federal government's vast housing and urban renewal program under Presidents Kennedy and Johnson, has pointed out: "The urban churches in the latter half of the nineteenth century in this country recognized that social evils were moral evils, and they provided the moral leadership that made possible the social changes of that period. The need for church leadership today is just as great." During the last forty years churches seem to have become so preoccupied with the affairs of their own congregations and their own institutional problems as to become cut off from the growing community problems around them.

Today the Church can be a part of the neighborhood effort in many ways. It can inspire and supply leadership. It can encourage physical improvements by modernizing and beautifying its own property. It can open up many of its facilities for community use, and it sometimes can supply money. St. Leo and St. Sabina parishes in Chicago have supplied thousands of dollars for the budget of the renewal association in their area, the Organization of the Southwest Community. Most basic, it can help its parishioners understand love and thereby open the way to sense of community.

Churches can train groups of their lay people in many of the skills needed for responsible neighborhood renewal work, just as they have trained lay people for charitable work and parish fund raising. Some churches and some clergymen in recent years have begun belatedly, to show forthright leadership in the movement for racial equality. Particularly in the suburbs the Church is in a position to show leadership where many people are fearful, weak, or blinded by prejudice.

In facing the awesome responsibility of relocating many families, urban renewal officials themselves have come to call upon churches for aid, asking that they work to modify some of the strains and stresses that can disrupt family life during forced moving. This can involve both guidance and counseling before a family moves, and efforts to secure a gracious reception for them in a new neighborhood. Some slum families need education to meet the higher standards of the neighborhoods into which they are to move. Programs of social education of this kind have been carried on by the Church of St. Matthew and St. Timothy in New York. This parish's housing clinics particularly have helped new rural immigrants.

A second part of the task is preparing existing residents to accept newcomers. The Catholic parishes in some changing old-city neighborhoods have probably done a providential service by opening their usually well-run schools to the children of newcomers, regardless of their religion. These children then have the opportunity to develop minds and character in an atmosphere of order and discipline not always found in the overcrowded slum public school with its high turnover of teachers and students. The stable, dedicated nun teaching in the parochial school can be a source of tranquility and inspiration for the slum child.

Many church denominations have large organized programs of social services, administered on a city-wide level. Mathew Ahmann, Catholic lay leader in church-sponsored interracial efforts, has commented on them thus:

"We should give more serious thought to how these social service programs can be used on a local neighborhood basis to meet the needs of an underskilled, problem-filled neighborhood. People here are not oriented toward downtown agencies; we should bring the programs to our parish centers, and open them to the total community there." He cites two such local social service programs, one operating in the "Corktown" parish of Father Clement Kern in Detroit; the other in Philadelphia's Gesu Parish. In several areas churches are serving as sponsors of nonprofit housing developments for the elderly.

Through active participation, churches have an opportunity to help neighborhood planning be done with full consideration for human and spiritual values. How effectively churches utilize this opportunity will only be known after many more neighborhood programs have been executed in various cities. No one feels it is the role of the church to give blanket approval to every renewal plan that is produced. But it is certainly the responsibility of the church to participate in formulating plans. Churches can make a contribution simply by being forthrightly critical, as the Archdiocese of Chicago has been.

When human values are ignored — as when plans might promote segregation or fail to provide housing for the income groups that need it most — then a church might find itself seeking changes in a plan. A neighborhood moves forward, however, when the various interests in it, including churches, can thrash out their differences among themselves and take a united position before the whole metropolis.

The role of the parish pastor is crucial. While it is not at all necessary — or perhaps even desirable — that he become a top leader in the neighborhood organization, his presence and participation are needed. When the pastor is seen and heard in the midst of struggle, then the church comes alive for people. They are given new courage and confidence. The church itself learns how it must reorganize itself, its time schedules and services, its counseling and education, its organizations, its whole relationship to the urban men of whom it would make a community. Pastors active in their neighborhoods often say that their sermons were ignored until they began to get out and personally experience the problems of the neighborhood — then their parishioners began to pay them heed.

Each metropolitan area has large numbers of churches that can enter deeply into urban life, and help untangle the disorder, repair the dilapidation. The Pittsburgh metropolis, for instance, has eighteen hundred churches and synagogues. Chicago has over twenty-four hundred churches and synagogues, Los Angeles two thousand, Peoria two hundred, Baltimore over eight hundred. There are sixty-four Catholic churches within the city limits of Baltimore, and thirty-three of them are in present or future urban renewal areas. And so on, around the nation.

Concern for parish participation in renewal is now evident in church affairs on the national level. The National Lutheran Church Council, one of a growing number of Protestant national organizations active in this field, states its view thus:

> The church is beginning to understand that many persons in high positions in government, business, and industry are keenly aware of the need for a better articulation of human and spiritual values in the building and rebuilding of our cities. The eagerness with which they respond to the overtures of the church stands in sharp contrast to the frequent aloofness of the church from the affairs of men.

> This is the opportunity and the challenge to the church . . . the rebuilding of our cities is not simply a problem of administration, economics and architecture. The city is one of man's greatest creations. As such it must, and will, reflect his innermost response to the love of God. . . .

Priests and laymen of the Catholic Church who work in some aspect of planning and urban affairs have been holding periodic national meetings to discuss urban problems. One of the major concerns of those participating has been assisting the parish church in solving the problems of the neighborhood around it. A number of dioceses have set up renewal and planning offices that are able to help parishes enter neighborhood work. Such offices in Washington, D.C., and Chicago have been particularly active.

A great deal is yet to be learned about the role of the parish church in neighborhood development. ACTION-Housing in Pittsburgh has sponsored an action-research project in cooperation with several denominations, looking at a Catholic parish, a Protestant church, and a Jewish synagogue, each in a different Pittsburgh neighborhood. This project has sought to determine the full potential of the neighborhood church for participation in community renewal efforts, within the church's mission. Consultant for the project has been Dr. Clifford Ham, former pastor of Baltimore's East Station Methodist Church, who is now a professor of city planning. Dr. Ham interviewed the pastor, or rabbi, and several laymen of each of the three neighborhood religious institutions under study, as well as leaders from the surrounding community. Some of the more significant findings were these:

> While clergymen and laymen of the three churches generally feel the church has a responsibility for neighborhood improvement, there is little precise knowledge about what to do. Within the Jewish congregation studied, "community" is narrowly defined to include only the Jewish group, and principally only the members of the congregation itself. Self-preservation and the continuity of the religious institution were apparently the strongest motivations toward community improvement in all three churches studied. The complexities of urban life have not been fully accepted by church leadership, so that emphasis on individual needs continues to predominate, with little attention to community needs. None of the neighborhood churches studied had clearly defined goals to guide future direction.

> Tensions were noted between racial and religious groups, socio-economic classes, newcomers and old-timers, renters and homeowners, and age groups. This was especially true when the newcomers were younger, child-rearing Negro families while the long-time residents were older, white homeowners of higher income. The members of the Jewish congregation took little interest in the plight of poor Negro families in the living area immediately adjacent to their synagogue, but were pleased with an urban renewal project which, as a byproduct, removed these Negroes to provide land for new middle-income apartments. The members of the Catholic parish showed resentment toward Negro families moving into their neighborhood. Members of the Protestant parish, Negro and white alike, wanted

nothing to do with public welfare families living near their church.

The three institutions all supported the citizen organizations in their neighborhoods in one way or another; other churches and synagogues nearby, however, had no contact with these organizations and in some cases were antagonistic and uncooperative. According to the clergy interviewed, the seminaries of all three faiths fail to teach their students about urban problems, city planning, housing, or urban renewal, and they fail to give any guidance in administering a city church or synagogue. Leaders of the three institutions studied had recruited few laymen out of their congregations for active neighborhood work.

Leaders of all three churches indicated that the denomination's central or diocesan office plays a relatively small part in stimulating neighborhood activities, although it generally encourages such effort once it is undertaken by a local church. The denominations seldom have a clear plan for the future of their churches; the pastor, by his own efforts and decisions, usually determines the future of the congregation.

Leaders of several denominations mentioned the need for more information and guidance on urban problems and projects. Good will, a desire to work for the betterment of the community, and resources are clearly available; lacking is technical knowledge, specific details, and the formulation of goals.

Some of Dr. Ham's major recommendations are:

Neighborhood churches—particularly through pastor or rabbi — should motivate able lay members to participate responsibly in citizen organizations. Churches can also train laymen for leadership, as some churches in the past have trained leaders for labor unions. Emphasis should be placed on social redemption as well as personal salvation; that is, churches should help their members gain a concern for racial equality, good housing, employment, welfare, and other essential needs, and seek to build a sense of community.

The church should take initiative to be sure it has a decisive role in formulating and evaluating neighborhood planning. Local churches should focus attention on the neighborhoods around them as well as on their members. Local churches should give major support to neighborhood organizations, including designating at least one member as an official representative.

Denominations should institute long-range planning to meet the needs of their churches. Denominations should select pastors for urban churches with great care. These men should be exceptionally well-qualified and motivated. They should serve for long terms, and receive special training as needed.

Seminaries should devote more attention to the metropolis and urban problems, with courses in urban politics, urban economics, urban renewal, planning, and sociology, taught by experienced laymen.

The religious institution's neighborhood role is summed up by these words of Father Joseph Meenan, pastor of St. Stephen's Roman Catholic Church in Hazelwood-Glenwood: "When dilapidated housing, racial tension, and unemployment bring on despair and spiritual blight, people are held back from salvation. The parish church has a great responsibility to act."

The Church enters the business of social services only because secular resources are sick or neglectful. The sooner these resources are adequate and well functioning the sooner the Church can concentrate on its central mission. This mission is set forth by Boston's Father John J. Harmon, Episcopalian priest: ". . . it is to celebrate the Eucharist, to nourish Christians in Scripture and theology, and to provide a constant stream of people who know themselves to be free in the Lord to respond to and bear the pain and joy of urban life — that is to live within it, and not outside of it. And whatever [service] programs do emerge should not be ecclesiastical but should reflect the fact that it is with and through those who bear the chief burdens of our social sickness that we all can see most clearly what and how things should be done."

As the Church begins to live within the whole urban environment, taking to itself the unpopular and repulsive as well as the respected and the comfortable, it will become a more decisive force in shaping that environment; people of the metropolis and its neighborhood will have an ally of the most effective kind.

The aid of the university is perhaps not potentially as significant as that of the Church, but is nevertheless great. The Church can help motivate man for active, responsible citizenship, and can help him gain the spiritual strength to sustain his effort. The university can help educate man for skilled, productive citizenship, and can continually supply him with new knowledge and ideas. In reaching out to assist urban people to unfold their full talents, to become alert and constructive urbanites, the university can do much to vitalize the metropolis. Many universities have wisely launched or supported programs to help renew the physical environment around their own campuses. These have included Columbia University, St. Louis University, Illinois Institute of Technology, the University of Chicago, the University of Pennsylvania, Duquesne University, and at least seventy-five others in large cities. Although this kind of action, which springs from self-interest, helps to revitalize the whole metropolis, it still makes only a limited contribution. There is a much wider participation for the university in urban rebuilding.

The urban university can share responsibility for the total development of the metropolitan community in which it exists, including giving assistance to individual neighborhoods. For the American university to help solve the special problems of this era of exploding urbanism is fully within the university tradition. Dr. Mason Gross is president of Rutgers, a university that has been in the forefront of assisting urban communities in the highly urbanized state of New Jersey. Dr. Gross has pointed out that the involvement of universities in urban problems is, "at once a normal development of the historic mission of American colleges and universities, and something quite new and exciting. . . . One of the accepted tasks of the American college and university from the very beginning of our tradition has been to meet certain of the more pressing needs of the community."

Universities can serve the community by providing it with graduates able to give professional leadership, by planning and organizing research to solve problems and discover new knowledge, and by extension services through which the knowledge gathered and discovered by the university can be brought to the wider community.

Rutgers, by the work it has done in Newark, offers a good example of the university as an urban ally. In cooperation with the mayor and the Board of Education the University has undertaken to determine why only a small percentage of students from predominately Negro neighborhoods go on to any form of higher education. The program was planned at the urban studies center of the University and involved not only faculty members but social and educational leaders of Newark. Reports are carefully assembled on high school students, their family background, financial condition, housing, job opportunities, intelligence, accomplishment in school programs from kindergarten on up, and their psychological motivation. Out of such a study Rutgers and Newark hope to establish a program to help neighborhood schools send more of their talented graduates to college.

Rutgers has received a Ford Foundation grant to make possible a broad program of assistance to urban communities throughout New Jersey. Other large state universities have received similar grants to finance ways of extending their resources out to the community. These "urban extension" grants make possible a number of demonstrations which are tying universities to urban areas around them.

The University of Delaware has been assisting cities in the organization of planning and urban renewal programs, particularly in Wilmington. It sends out an urban agent to assist smaller cities with such matters as annexation, budgeting, and how to take advantage of federal urban aids. These agents can help neighborhood groups. The University of Illinois has worked with leaders in Peoria, Rockford, and Springfield seeking to learn how the University's research skills can be put to work on race relations in public housing, downtown redevelopment, and the creation of urban agents.

The University of Oklahoma is educating "urban scientists" who can be the kind of staff generalists described in Chapter 8. These newly developing professionals learn to deal with the whole range of urban life. Upon graduation they will take positions with city government or urban development organizations working with all types of urban problems — in some cases on the neighborhood level. They have done intern work in such Oklahoma cities as Tulsa, Oklahoma City, Duncan, and Lawton under the sponsorship in some cases of city government, in other cases of a chamber of commerce or special citizens' committee.

At the University of Wisconsin there has been under way a conscious reorganization of the whole university to serve a state which has changed from one dominated by farm, forestry, and fishing to one predominately industrial and urban. The General Extension Service and

Agricultural Extension Service at Wisconsin are being combined into a single extension operation which will be primarily an urban extension service. Centers are being set up in the populous places around the state to provide instruction, research, and extension for the surrounding community, these centers being called "urban experiment stations," in the tradition of the agricultural experiment stations which in past times did so much to develop productive fertilizers, stronger breeds of cattle, and other improved farming methods. Working out of the new urban centers will be multidiscipline research-action teams for dealing with urban problems on a regional basis. The largest center, of course, is being developed in the Milwaukee metropolis, which has one-fourth of the state's population.

President Johnson has assigned his Commissioner of Education to make plans for an urban extension service as comprehensive as the federally supported Agricultural Extension Service. Said the President in announcing this project, "The needs of [urban people] are immense. But just as our colleges and universities changed the future of our farms a century ago, so they can help change the future of our cities."

One of the most direct ways universities already have been helping urban neighborhoods is through assignment of students to do field work with neighborhood organizations. In Pittsburgh, for instance, Duquesne University has not only had students in sociology assisting the people of Hazelwood-Glenwood in basic studies of their assets and liabilities on which to base planning, but other students from Duquesne have assisted merchants in Homewood-Brushton in marketing and merchandising studies. Carnegie Tech sends its student teachers out to Homewood-Brushton and other neighborhoods to assist with tutoring programs for slow learners. Its architectural students have aided Hazelwood-Glenwood people to plan new recreation facilities. The Graduate School of Social Work of the University of Pittsburgh has furnished field work students to assist several neighborhood efforts, and the head of its community organization division has served as an evaluator for the Homewood-Brushton program.

Western Psychiatric Institute, affiliated with the University of Pittsburgh, has set up a permanent experimental clinic in Hazelwood-Glenwood. Through this clinic, studies are being made in community psychiatry, focusing on school dropouts and the effects of automation and race tension on urban citizens. In the process Hazelwood-Glenwood has a powerful resource available, for the clinic staff is furnishing some direct mental health services to neighborhood people. As mentioned earlier, the Institute of Local Government of the Graduate School of Public and International Affairs at the University of Pittsburgh is assisting citizens in Perry Hilltop and local government officials to utilize modern advances in the science of public administration toward developing model city services.

All of these uses of university resources merely begin to tap the rich vein of resources that is in the universities. The urban university today is becoming one of the most powerful forces in the metropolis, a major employer whose needs are always expanding, a major builder, user of land, a major influence in the operation of local government. The metropolis depends upon the university as a research center and economic generator. In time the metropolis may be as much organized around the university as it is around the business-governmental-entertainment center we call downtown.

As an expanding center of power, wealth, and action, the university's responsibility for the community of which it is a part grows ever greater. The urban university can assist the metropolis and its neighborhoods in several important ways.

1. It can furnish well-educated graduates, competent in their fields, possessed of understanding of the new urban society, and of a sense of dedication, who can take on the multiplying planning and action jobs. There is great need for good lawyers, good planners, good doctors, good administrators, good communicators, good teachers, good men for all the other professions — men with an educational background relevant to the urban age. These men need not only high technical competence, but preparation for making the difficult social decisions that will face them.

2. The university can loan specialized personnel and furnish consulting services for urban development efforts. This may include furnishing urban generalists to direct neighborhood demonstration projects, student interns and trainees to assist neighborhood generalists plus specialized staff in such fields as educational research, shopping-center design, mortgage financing, landscape architecture, home economics, and the like. It may include furnishing advisory services directly to a community, as the University of Delaware is doing, or in giving assistance in dealing with juvenile delinquency as New York University does.

3. The university can provide special education for action people. This may take the form of: on-campus courses at night or on weekends; in-service training institutes for staff of renewal agencies and neighborhood organizations; leadership training and specialized courses for citizen volunteers and for special groups of professional people such as schoolteachers, settlement house workers, and policemen. It can bring courses and workshops to the neighborhood in political history and meth-

ods, in human relations, and a hundred important, relevant subjects. Community people can take part in some
regular university courses and in research projects. It
is perhaps as important that the community have its
agents bring experience to the university as the other
way around.

4. The university can do research to discover needed
new techniques for solving many urban problems and
taking advantage of many urban opportunities. The university can furnish the personnel to evaluate urban programs, a function of neighborhood renewal too often
neglected, with wasteful results. Research can involve
basic studies into such fundamental matters as motivation, mobility, race relations, communications, leisure,
neighborhood economics, social planning, urban democracy, and others. The university is often respected as a
disinterested expert in community conflicts and sometimes can help resolve them.

5. Publications are another aid from the university.
These can include training manuals, how-to-do-it book-
lets on home improvement financing, reports on various
kinds of urban research.

6. The university can enter the direct-action arena
with demonstration projects to show how a new technique can be used. Schools of education sometimes do
this with experimental teaching in a nearby grade school
or high school. Or a botany department may demonstrate
a hardy new kind of street tree in a neighborhood.

Political scientist Robert Wood points out the special
need for the university in our urban age:

> . . . our society . . . can be viewed as a Persuasive So-
> ciety. That is, it is community life organized and made
> cohesive by the capacity of men to enlist or co-opt
> the support of others, to change attitudes by educa-

tion or communication, to exercise influence increasingly by "the word. . . . "

In a Persuasive Society, the critical question is always whether or not information will be available, choices determined, and attitudes shaped on the basis of wide access to facts, reasonable analysis and reasoned debate. So, in great measure, the process of resolving our burning issues of civil rights, the ordering of urban space, the control of violence, the building of new communities, will turn on the vigor and excellence of university participation.

The potentially rich relationship between university and urban neighborhoods has hardly been explored, just as the depth of Church participation in revitalizing and renewing urban life has been little probed. In this modern urban age, when man's opportunities lie principally in the growth of mind and spirit, these are two allies to be sought eagerly and utilized with great enthusiasm. We find that some churches and universities have not yet turned outward toward their communities. Here the initiative of the urban operator, professional or volunteer, should not be spared. The whole urban community, as well as the Church and university themselves, have much to gain.

# Chapter 12

## THE INDISPENSABLE CITIZEN

One of the glories of American society is its democratic spirit. A major question that faces us in our time is whether this spirit will grow or decline amid the urban rush.

A book like Merle Curti's *Making of An American Community* shows us how democracy flourished in the small town and countryside of the last century. He tells the story of the settlement and growth of Trempealeau County in Wisconsin, and relates the wide participation of citizens in public matters. Farmers and shopkeepers, Curti tells us, would often leave their work for two whole days to sit in the town meeting and decide on road routes, bridge repairs, and the town budget. Citizens developed in respect and responsibility as they made decisions.

Today with our large populations and complex public questions of planning, health, education, welfare, taxation, employment, zoning, and the like, local government must be carried out by elected representatives and professional experts. The old-fashioned town-meeting method of making major government decisions is inadequate and impossible for the metropolis. There are, however, creative modern alternatives coming into being which in part fulfill the function of the old town meeting and help the metropolis perform its mission of producing an environment of dignity for people. These alternatives give the average householder an opportunity to move outward from his home and family to participate directly in public decisions. Whether the householder takes ad-

191

vantage of such opportunity is up to him. The democratic spirit demands that man be free to participate or not to participate, according to his own choosing.

The block groups of Hyde Park-Kenwood and the planning committees in Homewood-Brushton are examples of modern alternatives. Likewise, the spirit of the town meeting is very much alive when the Northwood Acres Association meets with its township council to debate sewer rates, or the Independent Voters of Illinois holds neighborhood meetings to argue the merits of candidates.

There are those who say that mere voting is participation enough. Eugene Rostow, the distinguished law dean and his wife Edna, writing in the book, *The Urban Condition,* edited by Leonard J. Duhl, state: "Democracy is an integrative community process of consultation, of dialogue, of forming of public opinion, and then expressing it through votes. So long as periodic voting remains the ultimate source of power, the principles of democracy do not confine us to the procedures of a town meeting. . . ."

The Rostows go on to suggest that perhaps citizens take to participation in neighborhood planning as "a welcome relief from the disturbing problems of the nation and the world. . . ." However, if the Rostows would look carefully at the leaders in the neighborhoods we have been discussing they would soon see that the men and women most concerned with democratic urban planning are the same citizens who are best informed and most concerned about national and world issues. Participation in neighborhood civic affairs, in short, is a prime producer of first-class citizens. This participation lifts sights and broadens viewpoints.

Voting is the basic act of democracy. And breathing is the basic act of life. But voting by itself does not make a developed citizen, any more than breathing alone makes a healthy body. Voting to elect a representative is at best impersonal and limited participation. The Rostows mention the consultation, dialogue, and forming of public opinion that lead up to voting. And these certainly make voting an intelligent process. But to stop at voting is to leave men isolated in the face of complex issues. A chief of government like General DeGaulle has used the referendum to impose a kind of benevolent despotism on France. He has made major decisions on complex issues by himself, then submitted them to the people for a vote. His overwhelming popularity carries the referendum his way, and the normal process of parliamentary debate is bypassed — and the issues are not decided on their merits.

The voting booth is a basic and absolutely necessary instrument of democracy. It is also a very lonely place. There is no community there. Man in our time makes his will felt most effectively by collective planning and group action. Neighborhood participation in public affairs is a creative effort wherein the individuality of the person can be expressed with endless variety. It is involvement beyond formal, legal, routine voting. It is a fuller citizenship.

Neighborhood development with its street redesigning, urban renewal projects, school revitalization, job training, home modernization, scientific police methods, and other activities deeply affecting the lives of families and neighbors, offers boundless opportunities for participation. People can come together in neighborhoods, in cities, in the whole metropolis, to discuss the problems and opportunities of their urban place. They can initiate plans and programs. They can review the plans and programs of officials. They can criticize, debate, reconcile. They can share in decisions. They can take action. They can block action. They can march and picket. They can applaud. In such interaction and community effort freedom flowers and becomes strong, people are educated, gain skills, and have their outlook and understanding broadened.

This participation not only helps the democratic spirit grow, but strengthens the urban development effort. The citizen's knowledge of his own neighborhood, his interest in it, and his imagination can often produce useful information and ideas for the professional planners. Participation helps public projects to meet the real needs of people. It motivates citizens to spend time, money, and effort helping carry out projects, as when they modernize their own homes in a conservation project. And it builds political support for well-conceived projects.

There are growing movements of political opposition to development today, especially against urban renewal. Yet only officials who accept citizens as partners in decision making can build the long-range political strength to keep their programs going. Without the citizen participation that took place in Hyde Park-Kenwood and Homewood-Brushton, the mayors and city councils of Chicago and Pittsburgh would have lacked the public support needed to adopt drastic plans for those two neighborhoods.

Decision-makers, public and private, are often reluctant about sharing their powers. Citizens can force open opportunities for participation, and the excitement of such conflict is often useful to arouse the general population to participate. Mothers in a number of cities have staged sit-downs at dangerous street intersections after officials had refused to consider suggestions for traffic changes. The attendant publicity has usually opened the way to serious consideration of the women's proposals, and aroused other citizens to interest in their neighborhood problems. In the long run, however, more is probably accomplished when the top decision-makers in government, business, and private organizations are sympathetic to participation, understand it, and welcome it from the beginning.

Public and private officials sometimes adopt a masterminding "we know what's good for you" viewpoint. Such attitudes are a serious barrier to neighborhood development and retard growth in the democratic spirit. In too many places decisions are made by officials behind closed doors. The decisions burst full-born and final upon a public which must live with them.

Expressway routes affect the lives of millions, rip up and crisscross neighborhoods and change work trips. They are often planned with little public knowledge. A proposed Lower Manhattan Expressway was laid out with little concern or communication with hundreds of thousands of persons affected. Engineers spent years planning it in the privacy of their offices, but it begot such opposition from so many organizations and individuals that it was finally killed by Mayor Wagner and the Board of Estimates.

Sometimes urban renewal projects, new schools, parks, convention halls come into being the same way. Plans for a new school that involved clearing several blocks of homes were proposed without participation in Baltimore's Harlem Park neighborhood; the uproar that ensued delayed the project for years and endangered an urban renewal project in the same area.

If a public work conceived without participation slides quietly through to completion without opposition, it may still fail to meet real needs. Some unused parks around the nation testify to this. Plans made without participation run two unnecessary risks: 1) they may not meet the real needs of people they are supposed to serve; and 2) even if they do meet real needs, they may generate political opposition and be delayed or destroyed.

Lack of participation in urban development results

from both the apathy and indifference of citizens (for the avenues to public planning are usually open to an alert citizenry) and from the inertia — sometimes the mastermind complex — of officials. When citizen participation is discussed in a gathering that includes officials of city hall, some official is bound to ask if elected representatives sitting on the city council and the citizen members of authority boards and planning commissions, do not provide all the citizen participation that is needed. This is what might be called a specious question. The obvious answer is "yes" until the question is examined carefully.

Consider the elected local legislator, whether he be called a councilman, commissioner, supervisor, selectman, or whatever. As a member of the governing body for a municipality he is charged by law with making certain final decisions. Likewise the members of authority boards and planning commissions make legal decisions. Councilmen, authority and planning commission members are not mere citizens. They are judges of what government must do. They sit above the various, contending citizen interests. For democracy to work in a complex urban society these interests must have their own spokesmen.

Suppose a group of citizens come before the council to ask for increased water pressure for their neighborhood. They are united, determined, and have but one interest in appearing. They make their case with maximum force, arguing from a simple, clear position. If they are enlightened they will have thought out their request in city-wide as well as neighborhood terms. The city councilman sitting in judgment cannot look at the issue in the same way. He has too many other interests he must consider. He must consider his relations with other groups. He must consider the effects of his decision on his fortunes in the next election. He must weigh what the newspapers will say. And he is often subject to direction from a mayor or other party leader. He cannot be the spokesman for every group on every issue. He can seldom argue with the same knowledge, force, and enthusiasm as the people who need the water.

There is a large communications gap between the public official and the citizen, a gap once filled by the town meeting. In the living areas of metropolis this gap exists in spite of community newspapers, legislative newsletters, and Sunday-night TV chats by the mayor. The public official seldom has a full view of what is in citizens' minds (although he often pretends he does) and the citizen seldom understands the variety of interests contending for the attention of the public official.

The neighborhood council with its committees and neighborhood meetings can begin to bridge the gap. The active presence at these meetings of public officials restores communications, and can help bring a "beyond-the-neighborhood" viewpoint to citizens in a local place. Participation is a school of leadership and, like all educational mechanisms, it can widen horizons and lift sights. If the mass of people are going to spend all their lives in homes, jobs, and bowling alleys, away from the decision-making places of the neighborhood and metropolis then democracy will wither. If enough people can move beyond their homes into the church basements, club halls and public hearings where neighborhood issues are debated, the democratic society will grow and the local community will be strengthened.

In Minneapolis, a system for establishing new neighborhood parks involves serious participation, with citizens sharing directly in the planning and financing.

Minneapolis families who feel the need for more play space in their neighborhood may suggest a new park to their PTA, church organization, or neighborhood council. If the group approves the idea, it will set up a committee to seek out a possible location, determine neighborhood desires as to kinds of equipment the park should have, and then approach the city park board. If the project appears feasible, the board makes preliminary sketches and cost estimates. The costs are apportioned among the owners of property in the area who will benefit, such costs usually running around five to ten dollars a year, per lot, for a period of twenty years. Supporters of the plan must go out and obtain the signatures of at least 51 percent of neighborhood property owners. Then the plan goes to the park commission for approval.

In Pittsburgh, the historic Duquesne Incline, whose little red cars carry passengers up and down Mt. Washington, fell into disrepair and financial difficulties in 1963. It was to be abandoned by the railway company which owned it. Neighborhood leaders of the Duquesne Heights Civic Association launched a fund-raising campaign, repaired the Incline, and today it continues to take residents to work, and serves as a major tourist attraction, with its hand-carved cherry paneling, handsome old hardware, and amber glass transoms restored.

Pittsburgh's war on poverty, being carried out under the Economic Opportunity Act which requires citizen involvement, is pioneering in formalized participation. A neighborhood citizens' group is the official channel of communications for the Mayor's Committee in each low-income neighborhood of the city. Any public or private agency bringing a new program into a neighborhood must work out its program in advance with the citizens' group, and submit to periodic evaluation as the program proceeds. (Homewood-Brushton and Hazelwood-Glenwood are two of Pittsburgh's priority neighborhoods for the Economic Opportunity Program.)

Necessary for any successful participation is information — particularly when complex projects like a neighborhood park or neighborhood renewal plan are

under consideration. Neighborhood communicators, as
described in the Homewood-Brushton chapter, can do
much in furnishing information to local people. Another
important medium is the newspaper — both daily and
neighborhood. It is certainly legitimate for a newspaper
to advocate a plan or project on its editorial page, but
in its news and feature columns it serves best by clear
presentations of facts and alternatives, with the views of
both opponents and proponents of a plan given space.

Excellent reporting of urban development is carried
on by the *New York Times,* the *Chicago Daily News,* the
*Pittsburgh Press,* and *Pittsburgh Post Gazette.* In the
neighborhood field the *Hyde Park Herald* in Chicago does
an outstanding job of keeping neighborhood people informed. These newspapers — and several others throughout the nation — have not held back in writing about
family relocation, forced moving of small businesses, rent
levels, neighborhood roots, historic buildings, race discrimination, political favoritism, and other issues in
urban development.

Participation is being informed, being able to ask
questions and get answers, being able to debate and discuss face-to-face with officials (whose technical competence must always be respected). It is careful examination of alternatives and even the formulation of new ones.
It is also the ability to accommodate and reach agreement, to give as well as take, to be positive as well as
negative, to arrive at a consensus for the common good.
The citizens' committee that merely fights all change is
as bad as the one that listens to the exciting words of
planners, looks uncritically upon plans, and gives automatic applause. Both kinds of committees are fakes and
frauds.

For citizens of a neighborhood to participate in urban
development requires an organization and committees.
It could not be otherwise in a complex society. But such

groups must be free, independent, and constantly striking at real issues. They must have in them representatives of all legitimate neighborhood interests. They must not be afraid of controversy, or of applying strong pressure in support of their views. At the same time that they are firm, they must also be reasonable and fair in dealing with other groups, including public bodies. The aim should always be improvement of the urban community.

The best long-run method is cooperative relationships, with militancy reserved for those times when the citizens' organization is completely frustrated in matters involving questions of justice. (Like the blockade in Hazelwood-Glenwood after twelve years of waiting for a promised new bridge.)

The East Liberty urban renewal project in Pittsburgh has had problems with relocation, problems typical of such projects, but this project also is a good example of citizen participation which built understanding and support for a project much needed by a depressed city. A year and a half of intensive information meetings, planning discussions, and negotiation sessions on specific problems preceded the beginning of the project, through cooperative effort between the East Liberty Citizens Renewal Council and the Urban Redevelopment Authority of Pittsburgh.

When the proposed project came before the city council for approval, the newspapers predicted an outpouring of bitter opposition from citizens. Instead, there were two days of informed, largely positive testimony by more than forty witnesses. Neighborhood people showed they understood the project and what it would do for their declining community. They also told how they had worked out certain changes in the plan with redevelopment officials. The drastic changes that urban development can bring are a great stimulant for forming neighborhood organizations. There are few motivators as effective as the bulldozer appearing on the horizon.

As pointed out in previous chapters, the most effective of neighborhood organizations are those which have professional staff assistance from some nongovernment source. The neighborhood staff organizer can help identify, recruit, motivate and educate citizen leadership. He can help it establish ties to the urban resources. He can help neighborhood people raise their sights from their own houses to the whole neighborhood and from the neighborhood to the whole metropolis.

The relation of the staff man to his neighborhood group is very important. He is neither master nor servant, but a leader. This relationship is strengthened when citizens have control over his hiring. In Hyde Park-Kenwood, the Community Conference raises all its own money and hires its own staff. In the Pittsburgh neighborhoods where the war on poverty is being waged staff coordinators are hired only after being interviewed and approved by the citizen-leaders of the neighborhood where they are to work.

The dedicated and skilled organizer gives continuity to citizen effort, helping it to sustain itself in the dry periods. The responsible staff man is self-effacing. He avoids the temptation to manipulate. One of his major goals is to help neighborhood leaders become wise, articulate operators, independent of himself. Basic community education for the citizen is an important service he helps to organize. Many urban experts feel it is citizen-staff brainpower and energy, more than new highways and housing projects, that are the keys to the attractive, prosperous, livable metropolis. The future of metropolitan neighborhoods depends on people, both those who enter the field of urban development professionally, and the citizen-leaders who become involved in the field part-time, to the limit of their abilities.

As neighborhood development proceeds, it becomes clear that there must be both a *what* and a *how*.

The *what* are the tools like urban renewal, compensatory education, manpower retraining, mobile health clinics, housing code enforcement, planned integration, and all the rest.

The *how* are the interest, dedication, faith, commitment of men, their sharing in decision making, opening their hearts, and building a sense of community.

The society that is a metropolis begins to develop well when it provides Joe Smith with a job, sound house, and good schools for his children. It begins to develop as a Great Society when it opens for him opportunities to be part of the deliberations and decisions of his own community, and provides the climate that helps make him willing to share his neighborhood and schools with men of all races and incomes.

The *what* is concrete and comparatively easy to get hold of; the *how* is amorphous and enormously more difficult. The *what* largely determines the health and prosperity of the urban place. The *how* largely determines the kind of citizens it will have.

President Johnson recognized the importance of the *how* in his 1965 inaugural address when he said, "If we succeed, it will not be because of what we have, but what we are; not because of what we own, but what we believe."

No social action program, no crusade against poverty, no movement of neighborhood development can make a great urban society without the *how*. The need for men to belong, to be engaged in decisions, to be masters of their own fate is reflected in the development operations of the federal government, now the most important partner of the metropolis. Before a city can receive federal urban renewal funds it must meet a workable program requirement that it have citizen participation in its urban renewal projects. And the Economic Opportunity Act states that local war on poverty programs must be, ". . . developed, conducted and administered with the maximum feasible participation of residents of the areas and members of the groups served. . . . "

Edgar and Jean Cahn, two lawyers who have worked in neighborhood development, state the case well in the *Yale Law Journal*:

> Poverty in America is not just a lack of material goods, education and jobs; it is also a sense of helplessness, a defeatism, a lack of dignity and self-respect. . . . It does not follow that the provision of services and the supplying of material wants will yield a sense of self-respect. And the elimination of want will not necessarily produce the kind of alert and concerned citizenry on which our democratic process relies. . . .
>
> In theory, the needs being filled are ones which will enable the recipient to become self-reliant, permitting the vicious cycle of dependency and helplessness to be broken. Yet, men with merchantable skills will not necessarily be able to or inclined to cope with the complex society in which they live, let alone participate effectively in the decision-making processes of that society. The mentality of despair, apathy, passivity, and the vulnerability to exploitation, harassment and manipulation will not automatically disappear because a vocational skill has been acquired. Indeed, reinforcement of those patterns may be the price which the customary donor-donee relationship exacts for the service or goods imparted. And this is perhaps the most serious cost of a service orientation: it neglects the poverty of the spirit in ministering to the needs of the flesh.

Citizen participation accomplishes two things. First, it is a process through which people can develop many of their talents and become responsible members of their neighborhood community. Second, it is an action tool for the social, physical, and economic revitalization of the neighborhood and the metropolis. Public renewal programs cannot move forward successfully without citizen support. On the other hand genuine citizen support cannot develop unless citizens have opportunities to know, study, evaluate, and contribute to renewal proposals, beginning in the earliest planning stages and continuing throughout the process.

In many neighborhoods where development programs are under way, and where there is seemingly considerable citizen participation, there are still thousands of citizens of low income and little education who are not being involved. One of the most important objectives of the war on poverty is to bring these people into active participation in organized urban society. In progressive cities the poor are being involved in planning war-on-poverty neighborhood programs, and the more talented among the poor are even being hired to help operate the programs.

Through citizen participation in neighborhood development efforts, democracy comes alive in the city streets.

# Chapter 13
## LOOKING FORWARD

This book began with the two primary facts of contemporary urban life; man, small and beleaguered, and the massive metropolis itself. Each has needs: man to grow and unfold his talents; the metropolis to achieve order and become an environment of dignity.

In many ways urban man shows traces of a rural origin. He likes to reside where there are trees and peaceful streets and people like himself. When he cannot find these things in his old city living area he pushes out to the suburbs. He wants to have shopping and schools close to home. He does not like government to be too remote. He needs peace and stability in surroundings he understands. As old inner-city areas are redeveloped there is a trend, shaped by the demands of man, to put into them not only high-rise buildings but green spaces, town houses with gardens, and compact shopping centers which lend themselves to people congregating and communicating. In old and new living areas citizens are demanding that schools become community centers.

Men still have a strong desire to possess their own piece of land. Today 63 percent of American families own the piece of land on which they live. Fifteen years ago this figure was 55 percent; sixty-five years ago it was only 47 percent. As the urban place grows larger, more complicated, in some ways more bewildering, man finds that one way to be stable in it is to have roots of ownership in a living area, even if a mortgage and periodic moving keep this ownership incomplete and unstable.

Man does not change nearly as swiftly as his inventions. Television, the expressway, and the jet plane may have him operating on a wider horizon, but he is far from relaxed on that horizon. He still desires a home and a place where he can put down roots. Studies by air lines reveal that three-quarters of the population stay close to home, while all the hurry-scurry of contemporary travel is generated by only one-quarter.

Through the last four thousand years man has clung to the small local community as one of his important connections to the planet. During this time there have been numerous revolutions of technology, manners, and morals. From these revolutions have come changes, but none of them has destroyed the usefulness of the local community. And the current revolution of automation and mobility is not destroying this usefulness either. The revolutions, current and past, have multiplied and altered human communities, with the local place — the neighborhood — remaining one of great importance. When properly developed, the neighborhood provides essential supports for the home, the focal point of growth for most men and their families.

Recent revolutions have transformed the neighborhood from a small self-contained unit to a sizable district linked closely to the larger urban place. They have brought the metropolis into being and generated great problems. If they are to have an orderly environment, urban people must solve these problems. Some of the most crucial are problems of poverty, lack of education, errant human conduct, physical decay, and disunity of people. These are so vast and hard to take hold of that easy, over-all solutions are impossible. Solutions require a logical breaking down of the metropolis into action areas.

Neighborhoods serve well as the basic action areas in attacking the great problems. They are the contact points for reaching and involving the poor and the alienated who are cut off from most of the institutions of metropolis. Here the local employment center, the mobile health clinic, the literacy class, and the housing improvement campaign can touch and bring to life the lost urban man. And here a supporting social system can be built to help man maintain stability, dignity, and a sense of belonging.

Social scientists have a word — "anomie" — for man's condition of being lost. To be in a state of anomie means living without any norms or values, unconnected to a social structure, in a kind of chaos. Urban society needs to set up imaginative, simple, new institutions through which lost man can discover and accept norms and thereby free himself of anomie. As we saw in the Homewood-Brushton chapter, the neighborhood citizens' organization, the local employment center, the housing clinic are among such effective new institutions. Man is most "found," is most secure and steady when he is building his own community, making decisions, assuming responsibility.

It is in the neighborhood — the good one, the functioning one — where man and metropolis meet. It is here that some of the most significant needs of each are taken care of. It is here that many of the basic human problems of metropolis are worked out. That the neighborhood is on the rise today is shown by its increased use as a planning and action base for the two largest development programs of our time. In nearly every metropolis, urban renewal and the war on poverty are being put to work neighborhood by neighborhood because this is the way the metropolis is put together. It is at the neighborhood level that people themselves join in such programs and give them vitality.

Increasingly, as the large modern neighborhood gains a sense of identity and an awareness of its problems, its need for direct, organized links to government increases. This need is especially felt in the large city where government is somewhat remote from neighborhood people. This need is met by a variety of new techniques including neighborhood planning boards, neighborhood city halls, representatives sent out from city hall, and the staff man of the neighborhood community organization, who often serves as a sort of local mayor.

Residents of suburban neighborhoods are coming to realize that the tiny municipality of which they are a part has inadequate resources to respond well to the needs of people; that there must be associations of local governments, to meet some needs like water supply, refuse disposal, and public transit. Some of these larger needs of suburban neighborhoods are so complicated that perhaps only some form of metropolitan organization can provide the resources to meet them.

It is conceivable, perhaps, that many years hence urban man will have no need for the local living area as a community, his knowledge and comprehension having become so great that he will understand the whole metropolis and be at ease in it. The metropolis itself will become his neighborhood, with children attending highly specialized schools anywhere in metropolis, with rapid transit systems putting every piece of metropolis within five minutes of every other piece, and with all shopping done in a few superefficient, low-cost centers.

Even if possible, such a one-neighborhood metropolis is at least several generations away. In the meantime we have the frightening problem of man being forced to live, ill at ease, in a complex society which is beyond his understanding. The present task is to build the district neighborhood well, to achieve in it the joint effort, the communication, the human attitudes of unity and responsibility which lead to sense of community — that fragile ingredient without which the neighborhood of today or the whole metropolis of tomorrow will be cold and unhappy.

A sense of community is an ingredient which only truly exists when it extends among and between all people — Negro and white, slow and brilliant, poor and wealthy. Racial apartheid is the strongest force acting against a sense of community. It is a divisive force based on emotion and therefore powerful and difficult to counter. It will be with us a long time; persistent and dedicated resistance, imaginative planning and action, sacrifice and courage are needed to eradicate it.

The neighborhood has a strong role to play for man and metropolis. But it does not serve them if its interest in home ownership and local services is introverted into a kind of isolationism. The good modern neighborhood is a secure springboard, not a hermitage. The neighborhood serves well when it freely opens itself to the world beyond. If it tries to close itself in — whether it is a suburban neighborhood closing out Negroes or an inner-city ghetto closing out planners — it will in time face agony.

An example of how planners, peering into the future, view the importance of the neighborhood to the metropolis can be seen in this goal taken from *A Plan For the Year 2000,* published by the National Capital Planning Commission in Washington, D.C. The plan calls for neighborhood communities with: ". . . a scale of environment which, while being extensive enough to have a distinct character, is at the same time sufficiently immediate and well defined to enable its residents to comprehend it readily and to identify themselves with it . . . each community within the District should also cultivate its own unique character as physical environment."

Powerful new forces are growing that will have a profound but unpredictable effect upon the urban future. Automation and cybernation may in a few short years make possible production of goods and services to meet the needs of all, with only a small number of the present work force employed. We could in a decade or two have a work force of more than one hundred million persons, with only fifty million jobs. We could meet this, as we are already beginning to do, with longer vacations, earlier retirement, keeping youth in school longer, creating a job corps, sabbatical leaves in industry, and a dozen other devices. We could come to the day when work will no longer be the central activity of men's lives. Philosopher Sebastian de Grazia in his massive study, *Time, Work, and Leisure,* looks to the day when leisure will become the central activity for the majority of men.

Drastic changes in how men spend their time will greatly affect the role and relevance of the urban neighborhood. Less work and more leisure for the present generation could mean more time spent at home, more time creating neighborhood fun — street parties, art fairs, children's activities; it could mean more property improvements and more time for joining in neighborhood development efforts. For far distant times it could mean more sophisticated people, more travel, and less interest in the home community. There is a trend in some new planned neighborhoods, like the retirement communities of the West, and the new towns of Reston, Virginia, and El Dorado Hills, California, to build neighborhood life around leisure activities. One of the most successful retirement communities, in Long Beach, California, is called "Leisure World."

Leisure will open the opportunity for more education. Men will have more skills and more time to make themselves masters of the planning that will continue to shape and reshape their environment, and thereby will be able to better control their own environment.

Developing technology will change the metropolis and affect its neighborhoods. Technology's greatest effect on the urban neighborhood will likely come through changes in transportation, with a variety of new forms of subways, monorails, skybuses, modernized suburban trains, and buses running in special express lanes. A Harvard Business School study predicts that really superior mass transit within metropolis will decrease pressure to own automobiles and give the urban citizen greater financial freedom. He will rent a car at the corner gas station for out-of-town trips. Less in-city driving will ease tensions, and provide more time for reading, conversation, and thinking. This could lead to a more learned, relaxed, responsible citizenry able to contribute more to the building of the community.

There are many other forces which will affect the role of the neighborhood. The effects of none can be predicted with certainty. What can be said with certainty is that most urban men will remain for some time in need of a local community, and that the effort to create strong modern urban neighborhoods is a work of great significance for present generations.

There are already over one billion urban men in the world. In thirty-five years there will be over three billion. In time there may well be only urban men on this planet. The mission of these men on earth is to serve God by developing their full human dignity. A great task before us is to build an urban environment that contributes to this dignity. For a very long time a major element in that environment is going to be the urban neighborhood.

This book has been written as part of a continuing search to discover the full usefulness of the neighborhood in modern urban life. This has been an interim report on that search. Much is yet to be learned and tested. It is hoped that many reading this book will have reactions, insights, suggestions that can help advance the search. The author would like to hear from such people.

# INDEX

## A

Abrahamson, Julia, 85
Accessibility
  between neighborhoods and central core, 67
Action for Boston Community Development
  community development organization, 116
  method of operating, 126-127
  work in South End, 46
ACTION-Housing, Inc.
  Church study, 179-182
  East Hills Park, 134
  neighborhood urban extension approach 117, 133-139
  sponsorship of Spring Hill Gardens, 88-94
  work with Homewood-Brushton neighborhood, 147-156
Adams, Richard M., 154
Agostinelli, Floyd, 36
Agricultural Extension Service, 126, 186
Ahmann, Mathew, 177
Alabama, 172
Alinsky, Saul D.
  founder of self-determination approach, 128-133
Allegheny Council to Improve Our Neighborhoods-Housing, Inc.; see ACTION-Housing, Inc.
Allegheny County (Pa.), 107, 133
  Health and Welfare Assn., 147-148
American Bar Association, 70, 159
American Public Administration Service, 70
American Society of Planning Officials, 31-32
Anacostia (Maryland), 36
Anomie, 207
Apartheid
  against sense of community, 209
  city-suburban separation of races, 15, 163
  living area as final stronghold, 88
  Negro gray area, 55
Archdiocese of Chicago
  opposition to Hyde Park-Kenwood plan, 78, 172, 177
*Atlanta Constitution,* 162-163

Aurora (neighborhood), 24
Automation, 209

## B

Back of the Yards Neighborhood Council, 128, 144
Balanced community, 96, 155-156
Baldwin Hills (California), 31
Baltimore
  East Baltimore Station Methodist Church, 174
  Harlem Park neighborhood, 30, 31
  Homeland neighborhood, 56
  Negroes reclaim neighborhoods, 45
  number of churches, 178
  South East Council for Community Services, 174
Baltimore & Ohio R.R., 110-111
Banfield, Edward C., 165-166
Banks, Sanford, 98-102
Battles, Clyde, 46
Beacon Hill (neighborhood), 56, 165
Beauty, 164-166
Bel Air (neighborhood), 24
Beverly Hills (neighborhood), 24
Bloomingdale (neighborhood), 24, 117, 121
Board of Public Education (of Pittsburgh), 150
Boston
  Action for Boston Community Development, 46, 116
  Beacon Hill neighborhood, 56, 165
  Charlestown neighborhood, 37
  Harmon, Father John, 182
  neighborhoods of, 24, 126
  non-profit development organization set up in, 123
  old streets, 14
  operation of development organization, 126-127
  Redevelopment Authority, 46
  social invention approach, 116, 123, 126-127
  South End neighborhood, 45-46
Boulden, Robert, 154
Bridgeport (neighborhood), 30
Brightwood Park Methodist Church, 173

KILROE SEMINARY LIBRARY
HONESDALE, PA.